INCONVENIENT CONSCIOUSNESS

What's next for humanity?

BY LORINA

First Published – 2025
This edition published 2025 by Lorina
Australia
Copyright © Lorina 2025

The National Library of Australia Cataloguing-in-Publication

Creator: Lorina, author.

Title: INCONVENIENT CONSCIOUSNESS / Lorina.

ISBN: 978-1-7637386-0-7 (paperback)

Subjects:	Non-fiction
	Consciousness
	Spiritual awakening
	Self-discovery
	Soul purpose
	Universal law

All rights reserved

This book is a work of non-fiction.

This book is sold subject to the condition that it shall not, by way of trade or otherwise, be lent, resold, hired out, or otherwise circulated without the publisher's prior consent.
All rights reserved. No part of this publication may be reproduced, stored in or introduced into a retrieval system, or transmitted, in any form, or by any means (electronical, mechanical, photocopying, recording or otherwise) without the prior written permission of the publisher. Any persons, who do any unauthorised act in relation to this publication may be liable to criminal prosecution and civil claims damages. The author asserts her moral rights. Only permissioned users are allowed to copy book pages for educational purposes.

Typeset in Times New Roman 12pt
Cover artwork by Susan Art
Original image by Susan Art at 99 Designs
Printed and bound in Australia by Ingram Spark

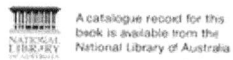

DEDICATION:

Within the human psyche of every single one of us, has been placed an energy in the name of thought forms of war and separation. This is non-benevolent action which began eons ago and was instigated by those less than interested in our greatest potential and more interested in gaining control of the planet. Many movies, including Star Wars, depicted the light and the dark forces and throughout earth's history this battle has been in progress. I don't intend to give this my focus but rather just to give you, the reader, some background of how we ended up here.

The universe has laws that govern creation. When a group of beings' intentions are self-focused, it lowers their vibration and capacity to expand and create. This essentially and inevitable protects the rest of the cosmos even as these beings play out their experience of fear and separation. This drop in vibration took our planet earth back to a third dimensional reality, a planet of separation and polarity. Judgements of right and wrong, good and bad, high and low and dark and light etc, has created separation of each other and within the belief of creation itself.

In understanding the past, it helps us make sense of where we are going and why we are experiencing so much turmoil particularly at the moment. Our planet and our human species are moving from the third, through the fourth, into the Fifth Dimension. Let's just look a little deeper into this battle and ultimate shift, to understand ourselves at a deeper level.

These war and separation thought forms that are played over and over in our minds and perpetuated through the conditioning of thinking via mainstream media, historic records, many religious groups, cultural/family conditioning etc, rule our planet or have, up until now. Just as any thought that we repeat turns into a belief, so too did these beliefs run our unconscious mind and that mind has largely run our bodies, our lives and our planet. Everything changed since we disconnected from our true selves. These negative thought forms are not a benevolent trait, rather one endowed upon us from those who oppose the light, truth and oneness. It has led us to this mess we find ourselves in today.

It set people against each other, created competition energy and fear of survival. It set humans against nature and our environment, against animals, man against women, man against man, women against women, them against them, us against them, it set country against country, it created wars, pain, poverty, destruction, even horrific neglect and death of our children. May this be a reminder as the elders of our planet, we are caretakers and responsible for the next generation. There is no species on earth that abuses their offspring, such is the depths we have fallen into and the disconnection from our hearts.

Our planets' destiny has always been very different to this, and most of us are aware of this truth. Asking ourselves, "is this really the best we can do?" Regardless of the struggle, there is exquisite beauty all around our planet that many of us can see is worth protecting.

In order to create change we must face this and wake up to what needs to change. As painful as that can be, we have to look at what we don't want to see. There is no other way.

Doing what we've always done will get us more of the same. Things intensify to get our attention. These thoughts and beliefs lie beneath all of the unbearable suffering and devastation that has, up until now, been the predominant story of planet earth.

The result of this unconscious driver is that our consciousness shifted from unity and peace to war and separation. In losing connection with our essence, we thought we were the voice in our head, and that we have been abandoned and are all alone. This fear-based reality cannot continue to grow because it's simply not the truth. Love and unity are based in truth and this illusion of separation is a fear-based program which brings with it devastating pain. It's an experience that most of us are ready to move on from.

Many of us have already become conscious that we are much more than the voice in our head, and that feelings and oneness are the key to our survival. This book is designed as a guidance for you, the reader, to gracefully make this shift back to what your heart and soul long for and already know.

This belief in separation has stunted our growth as a planet, due to isolation from our true selves, each other and the rest of the universe.

If we keep to ourselves and don't push ourselves up against each other and the support that is available throughout the universe, then our evolution stops. As we all do the work to own these parts of ourselves, the wars will end, the children will be protected and lovingly contribute their sacred missions for our new earth. The suffering will end, and we will return to our innate nature of love.

This is done by each of us recognising this warring part of ourselves. The part that wants to argue, judge, condemn, steal, take, fight, blame and even kill ourselves or each other. Once this is owned, it loses all power then we can return to unity and peace, where each of us become a global citizen and live the life intended for us here on planet earth. As we do that, owning and loving all of ourselves, we can then ascend into the fifth dimension, our New Earth of love and unity.

My intuition confirms to me there will come a great flash of light that will help us in this shift. Many people around the world have also channelled this information and made predictions about it, the name usually given to this is a solar flash or solar flashes. There are prophecies of three days of darkness which precedes a great change on earth; as always, I suggest you do your own research.

Much of this information is channelled from higher dimensional beings including angels and some from my feelings as a seer: it seems to me in regard to the flashes, the first and largest flash will occur during a time of great upheaval on the planet and will be followed by several more.

Their purpose is to more rapidly bring in a change in perception and to bring us together. By all counts, these flashes will change everything more rapidly than anything else has been able to and light will flood the planet like we have never experienced.

Our bodies are designed to hold more light than we have been currently holding, which I talk more about in the final chapter, but as we make shifts in our vibration this is changing. We as a species seem stuck in this war of separation perception and this flash of light event is an opportunity, to help those of us who are open at any level, to see, feel and embody our oneness.

I don't know how this will happen, but I feel most strongly that it will. No-one can know with certainty when this will occur, it is a design of creation, but it will be in divine timing, when everything lines up and our collective energy is ready. To me it seems imminent, a knowing that I have that goes beyond logical proof. It may even happen this year but free-will makes it impossible to pin point, it depends on our collective readiness. In this event everything will change, more light means more clarity and when we can see clearly, we make new and empowered choices. Our whole perception changes, which changes everything.

This message offers you a formula for preparation and awareness to see beyond the veil, this veil that covers our world that consists of our limited five sense data, that is very thin now. From this place my knowing is; both individually and collectively, bravely and uniquely we will walk home together. Each of us, a microcosm of the macrocosm.

Many of my views here are from personal exploration, spiritual connections and experience which I trust implicitly. They are not meant to represent an academic perspective.

I dedicate this message in deep gratitude to my compassionate, wise, courageous, thoughtful, loving and authentic children and grandchildren who are some of my greatest teachers and whom I love infinitely. Nathan, Stacey, Annique, Tess, Ben, Collins, Henderson, Mackenzie and those angels still to be born.

I include a big thank you to Alli Sinclair, who's skills include being an amazing author, editor, documentary producer and screen writer. She has encouraged me to share this information and passion, when I still had doubt in my abilities and the reception this work might receive. Her loyalty shows me the power of love and positive suggestion. How a friend's unwavering belief at just the right time in our lives, can change everything.

Lastly, I acknowledge all of you who have found or are searching for the courage to face yourselves, to learn to love all of it and to be all you came here to be. You who have the passion, dedication and love required to assist in shifting the collective of humanity to unity and love, our New World. We could not do this without you.

THOUGHTS FROM THE HEART

Tread gentle, be kind
Let your feelings guide your mind.
This process is precious, courageous and true
Treat it like a new born, who dwells within you.

As all that is not real, drops away
There'll be struggle and pain along with some play.
With surrender and release we begin to trust
Fear is illusion and our eternity a must.

We came with amnesia of who we are,
To travel this journey, near and far.
Lifetimes unfolded until we felt the call,
To find our way home, past the fall.

To reveal your essence, you must learn to feel
All that is not invited on our journey to heal.
Uncovering a gift of the highest decree
That all of us are love, that's that truth of you and me.

Darkness is the absence of light, not real and soon out of sight,
As fear is the absence of love; the higher-self you from above.
In absence of truth our soul cries, bound by restrictions that do tie,
We call upon our courage within, to set ourselves free so all will win.

So, take my hand and I'll take yours,
You are my family, feet and paws.
The ocean and the trees, the whales and the gnomes.
It's our time to link arms and together we walk home.

LORINA

CHAPTERS:

Introduction 1

Chapter 1   What is consciousness? 4
Chapter 2   Who is this shift for? 26
Chapter 3   What is "The great awakening"? 41
Chapter 4   Life happens for me and through me,
                not to me 63
Chapter 5   Sensitive people are the frogs
                of our planet 85
Chapter 6   Shifting dimensions:
                Embodying soul 150
Chapter 7   Manifestation and how it works 177
Chapter 8   Love, the very essence of creation 197
Chapter 9   The meaning of life leading us home 233

Summary 262

INTRODUCTION

Understanding consciousness is no more complicated than understanding the progression of life in the universe, that is, essentially, understanding universal law. This law is metaphysical therefore it is indestructible and infinite. Yet, in our conditioned societies, we have been taught that unless the mind can understand a concept or prove the existence of it in the physical world, it is invalid, weird, and does not deserve our attention or even our consideration.

We have, for a very long time, since the more advanced societies on our planets ceased to exist, been limited in understanding the magnificence of the human journey and our mind/body/energetic systems. The journey humanity has travelled from living consciously in unity and love to where many people are living or struggling to live today, is quickly coming to an end.

Humanity has been conditioned to place our power outside of ourselves and we are waking up to the disempowerment of this way of life. The health system, including big business pharmaceutical, many forms of government, many religions, the banking and education systems to name just a few, are in crisis and in fast time becoming redundant and unacceptable. They were supposed to be designed for the good of humanity, this is no longer the case. In the past when a store opened its doors, it was offering service to the community, to the public. That is no longer the intention of most of our structures.

Then shares were sold to generate more money, and the shareholders became the focus of the business. Everything that was for the good of the community was replaced by being focused on profit for the shareholders, even at the expense of the customers, community and the employees who lost their value too. This is just as true for banking, when they began their original intention was to support growth of a community until profit became their number one focus. Now people lose their houses, businesses and independence, as well as their health and desire for life, all for the sake of profit. We have literally taken this self-centred and separate paradigm to its brink.

Consciousness is a part of life, a part of evolution. It is a level of awareness that propels us to new perceptions. Everything in the universe is in the process of either being created, preserved or destroyed.

This process allows room for change and expansion of experience and without it there would be no order. Imagine creating and preserving things without the dissolution of them. Imagine preserving and dissolution of things without the creation of more or any combination without the three parts. It simply wouldn't work.

Amongst our purposes for being here on planet earth is the purpose of growing through knowing ourselves. To know the fullness of who we really are and then to embody that.

You will notice at the end of each chapter, a list of questions aimed at reflection of the chapter you have just finished. These questions and answers can expand on your own clarity and understanding of where you are at in your own journey or serve as a guide to where you would like to be. There will be a platform created where all of my readers can connect and discuss their questions and journey. See the end pages: Where to from here?

If you've ever considered there might be more to this

life than the mundane survival and slave routines that we have been conditioned to follow, that is your innate desire for truth and passion and for expansion wanting to be birthed.

At this unique time on earth, things are changing both on the inside of us, where everything must begin, as well as within the collective. The last place we will see this change is on the outside of us, in our lives, communities, and businesses. As the increased levels of light flood the earth and the light shines on the dark to expose it, we are shown what has become redundant and is no longer working. It shines on our wounded or shadow selves that have been holding us back through a belief in needing protection, to uncover who we really are and what we truly deserve. It really is an amazing time to be here.

There is much of the population that is still consciously asleep, those people who are just going through the motions, caught up in the rat race and in a trance of apathy.

There are waves of people waking up at all different stages, from the beginning, all the way to enlightenment and beyond because our growth is eternal. In chapter five I cover these waves of people in more detail. This book, I trust, is for those of us who are in the first wave and cutting the path for those who follow, for those waking up and for those curious about the possibility of something more for their life. Stay tuned the adventure is about to unfold…

CHAPTER 1

WHAT IS CONSCIOUSNESS?

This consciousness that I speak of is an energy like all things are and energy differs through the frequency of its vibration. Some things vibrate at a lower, slower and denser frequency and other things a higher, faster and lighter frequency. For example, a rock such as basalt is low, slow and dense in vibration and citrine crystals are high, light and fast in vibration. Just as people who have cleared fear and density from themselves are of a lighter energy, happy, positive, loving and can hold more light. This light is in its essence; information that the mind, body and spirit receive. It is truth, it is life force energy, it is clarity, it ignites our inner knowing, it is love. With this light flooding onto the planet comes the opportunity of consciousness, empowerment and unity.

This energy that I'm referring to as consciousness is the seed of power and remembrance that lies deeply within us all. It is impartial and unemotional, and it is ours to experience and learn about if we so wish to understand life's deeper meaning. Love is another word for consciousness.

It is the energy of consciousness that allows human kind to become aware of themselves as a part of something much larger. We can only become aware of the voice in our head because there is a part of us that observes it. *This observer is our true self,* some refer to it as our soul or higher-self. The part of us that is always present, always guiding us and always loving us unconditionally. This soul-self knows you deeply and completely.

It knows your intentions for this life, it knows your strengths and perceived weaknesses, it knows any contracts you have made to yourself or others. It knows the path of least resistance for your life but above all it loves you and supports your free will to make your own choices, even if we choose to ignore its existence.

Following your soul's direction in your life is consciously connecting to the power of the Universe: Mother/Father God, Source, the Divine, whatever you prefer to call it. We have played out an experience of being separate from this source of everything, through the collective belief in separation but in truth we have never been separated, except through our thoughts and conditioning.

As you reclaim this conscious connection to your source energy, it allows you to become aware of the immense power that you and each of us hold. As we are in truth, creator sparks and we are more capable and brilliant than we have ever been told. We have been kept in the dark up until now. The energy of the universe that is within us and all around us, responds to what we mean, not to what we say or even what we do. **The universe responds to intention**: we are creators of intention and that is why self-focused or fear-based intentions lead to pain and separation, while loving intentions lead to unity, joy and peace on earth.

There has been just one path on our planet for many thousands of years: the Karmic path. Now there are two: the Karmic and the Dharmic path. The Karmic path is one of separation and fear, based on how we judge ourselves and each other and a path where we learn through experiences of pain from the past. The Dharmic path is one where we live in alignment with our innate spiritual nature of oneness and love.

We continue to grow and learn but this happens in the present moment of our life, through acceptance and compassion. Ever since the belief in separation has run this planet our earthly journey has been one of healing the self, which moves us to an awareness of self-love so we can then love everyone else. This awareness of the true-self is the essence of consciousness and the return to oneness.

As children, we are born with thoughts and feelings that are limitless because our mind and bodies are in a pure state. Most of us know the feeling of holding a baby, they are pure love. Even young children often attempt the seemingly impossible, unaware that they have any limitations, physical or other. They are not yet fully embodied, and this takes many years. They have been known to climb to extreme heights or even run up to a random dog without fear. It's only later when they develop a sense of the physical-self around the age of seven years and with education and conditioning that they begin to learn the limitations of the human experience and physical body.

As we travel through life, we experience and learn many different things. Our mind develops ways of coping and thinking and we form beliefs about ourselves, those around us and give our world meaning. These confines and limitations, often carried on for generations, are generally just that, limited beliefs and fears, born from the meaning the individual has placed on a situation.

Nothing means anything until we give it a meaning: A rainy day is just a rainy day until we make it mean, for example, if you are a wedding planner: "It's a disaster, rain spoils everything" or if you are a keen gardener: "It's a great day for the garden". It's just a day with rain. The negative meanings and beliefs we give things are often brought about by feelings of disempowerment, misinformation and family and social conditioning.

For example, each child from the same family will leave that family with their own set of beliefs from their unique experiences and meanings, even though they lived in the same environment with the same parents. A thought that we have over and over forms a belief and that runs our unconscious mind just like a program would run a computer.

Our unconscious mind instigates around ninety-three percent of our thoughts, beliefs and behaviours and often they are limited beliefs and thoughts born from a thought pattern developed in situations where we felt unsafe, confused and where our needs were not met. They come from limitation and ignorance and result in disempowering feelings and behaviours. These limitations can be passed on through our ancestorial heritage, through parental modelling and unconscious beliefs that we often develop as a young child. They can also be instigated by traumatic events, society programming, genetic molecules /our DNA and sometimes they come from our past life cellular memory.

It would seem we have had endless opportunities to traverse the Karmic path and to learn from that. It has also become increasingly evident in my work as a Clinical Hypnotherapist, that it matters less where these limited beliefs came from and more that we acknowledge the existence of them and how we feel about them and then make the decision to let them go. This step then allows them to move from the unconscious mind into our conscious awareness. Once we acknowledge their presence in our life, we then have the freedom to make a change.

Once we become conscious of anything, it moves out of the inner mind or unconscious mind and into our everyday conscious awareness, from the shadow-self into the light of our everyday expression. We own it as a part of our experience. Everything you have done has value and given you experience and wisdom.

We cannot unknow something once we know it consciously. We can, however, be resistant to change and this is more of the Karmic path and will cause us more and more pain until we surrender to our soul's path. Typically, humans will only make a change when the pain of staying the same is greater than the pain of change. This willingness to surrender can take lifetimes for some people and may have for yourselves in some areas of your life but that's the beauty of free will, it's entirely up to you. We can pretend to make a change to appease another, but nothing will actually change until we decide to surrender. The universe cannot force you; some people prefer the addiction of the lower states of ego and want to sleep a little longer. It's entirely up to you.

You can make quantum leaps or progress as slow as a snail would, it's entirely up to you. It's all you, every perception of your life is created by you and your life is the result of your perceptions. Stay stuck or move forward, believe that the world is cruel and haphazard or believe the world is wise and compassionate. Whatever you believe, you perceive, and it <u>will</u> be your experience, every time without exception.

Knowing of our oneness; "I am you and you are me", leads to us caring for everyone and everything and another benefit is that our personal perceptions affect the collective. That is oneness is motion, it is a consequence of our evolution. Of course, there is no condemning creator who judges us, ever, we are only ever loved for all that we are, without conditions. There is, however, a responsibility for how we choose to progress.

This is not about guilt tripping anyone into certain behaviour, its more about understanding the power you hold to affect your environment and in fact the entire world and beyond. That's how much you matter, how valuable you are. Your life matters.

Carl Jung was a Swiss psychiatrist, psychotherapist and psychologist who founded the school of analytical psychology. He called this "collective consciousness" and it seems to gain validity as it moves through time. We can see from later generations who experience a life that was rigid, domineering and restrictive and as a result, their lives became a life of disempowerment and struggle. In many institutions we are still being told by those people who have lived before us, (either in text or in person) who lived in a very different environment, with very different beliefs; how we should live today. These people who believe the mind and that only physical proof is where wisdom resides, tell us what we are going to experience in life and what we and our body is capable of. They do this with an unspoken promise, "This is how things are and that's all there is to it."

It's a bit like going back to when you were six years old and using what you learnt then, now. Everything has changed and it's no longer relevant. It is negating our development, progression and evolution and it has kept us stuck for long enough. Would you agree?

It has taken humankind thousands upon thousands of years to be dulled down and fall asleep. To stop questioning those things that don't feel right or to think for themselves from the present moment, and to be where many people are today.

So many of us have given away the responsibility to govern our own lives and this has come at an enormous cost to ourselves, to each other, and to the planet.

The history of our planet shows that we have moved between ages: the dark age and the golden age. The dark age is a time when there is control of information, cohesion, powering over, less freedom, control of resources, separation consciousness, dark technology and slave mentality/sweatshops/child labour and the likes. The golden age is one where we experience living as our true selves with our psychic abilities, a heart centred ecosystem, abundance consciousness, enlightenment, clarity, unity, knowing oneself, spiritual awareness where we act in respect of natural laws: such as all beings are inherently free.

There are no surprises here, but I believe it's important to be aware and name it. As a collective we are coming out of a dark age and moving into a golden age. There is something unique about this approaching golden age, it's destined to go all the way to the Fifth Dimension. The main difference this time for those of us choosing to partake, is there is no returning to the dark age. This is monumental and *every one of you* is an important ingredient.

We have to meet the universe half way by firstly owning and loving all of ourselves and secondly by treating all beings as inherently free, while doing unto them as we would have them do to us. The universe will then align us to opportunities that guide us on this ascension path.

Please know that spark of brilliant light still burns in every single one of you and is calling you to own it louder than ever before. Do you know it? Can you feel it? Can you hear it? Can you sense it? Do you see it?

This is the time of the ascension where the earth and her inhabitants- us humans, (as most animals and nature are already living in the Fifth Dimension)- have the opportunity to return consciously to our true magnificence or God realised self, known as the fifth dimensional (5D) reality. The ascension as I understand it, will not be as Jesus did when he left the planet in his body. He was already an ascended master and that was a different time.

My sense of it is that most of us, if not all of us, (in this first wave at least) will ascend energetically and stay here to complete our mission. The shift happens vibrationally from within as we shift into a new perspective which changes everything in our experience, while remaining here on earth.

This ascension process is one where we embody our inner truth and souls knowing, that we are love and that we are all one. As we do to another, we do to ourselves. That we are capable of self-generation and self-healing and that we are conscious creators living in the knowledge that the human being is so much more than we have been told. Many of us have heard this before from the spiritual teachers that have visited our planet but the time has come to live it.

The guidance these masters (not gender specific) gave us has not been easy to access for example: much of Jesus' teachings were left out of the bible by those wanting to limit our potential and capacity as human beings. However, please remember no thing is stronger than the light and as the light unveils the truth, it will prevail. Truth always comes to the surface eventually. We have guidance in many forms flooding the planet at this time, because it is time and the only happiness and fulfilment is found in aligning the personality or ego-self with the soul.

That's where this ascension path is leading you and from here. We will live a life of joy in unity, authenticity, wholeness and love.

In order to accomplish this monumental shift, the ascension into the Fifth Dimension while living in physicality, things will need to get messy as birth of the new usually does. Have you noticed messy happenings on our planet of late? The ascension from the Third Dimension (3D) has never been successfully accomplished while still living in a human body before, but now it is for those who choose it because now is the time.

We have been given information by many masters who have lived before on our planet, such as Ram, Krishna, Buddha, Mother Mary, Jesus Christ and Mary Magdalene his twin flame and Meher Baba and more. They told us of our magnificence and that we too could do the things they did and even gave us details as to how to achieve enlightenment or self-realisation. With all of this information there is still no clear pathway for this ascension process because it is unique, we are literally making it up as we go.

My question to you is: Do you want more? Do you feel you are not living up to all you can be? Without the latest new thing or relationship or the next holiday, without that thing you are addicted to, is this enough? Are you truly happy from inside of you?

Lemuria is an ancient civilization that many believe is the original Garden of Eden or Motherhood of humanity. This large island was situated around North America, and included parts of Africa, Madagascar, India, Easter Island, Hawaii and Northern California. It was a civilization where people lived in harmony and possessed a sophisticated technology that allowed them to harness the weather, defy gravity and heal themselves. They also communicated through telepathy and a heart/star/light language that they understood innately. They used water and crystals as sacred healers and lived in a love-based reality. These beings came from all over the universe:

from Sirius, Pleiades, Arcturia, and many smaller planets. It was a coming together of many civilizations where they interbred for a few million years to create an original seed of human for the planet, heaven on earth. This was the original plan for earth.

The Lemurian age ended somewhere around 50,000 years ago give or take, depending on who's presenting the research, with what was reported to be a thermal blast that sunk the island almost overnight. They lived in fifth dimensional reality and being aware of their impending demise, used ancient crystals and vibration to hollow out an underground city beneath Mount Shasta in California. This was said to be a place to preserve artefacts, their culture and wisdom.

There are many ancestors of original Lemurians living in these areas today, this civilization is preparing for the 5D shift of humanity and is seeded through what is known as the volunteers.

There are Lemurians who chose through free will to come back for many, many lifetimes, to be here now for the raising of consciousness to 5D. I suspect we didn't really know what we were signing up for, no one could predict a world of free will and it hasn't been for the faint of heart but somehow, we made it.

My connection to this place is unmistakable and I have more recently activated a star language which I recognise as possible being Lemurian, from the information I have researched. My sense is this language may go beyond Lemuria and originate from another star group or other planets where I spent many lifetimes. Many of us have a star language that can be activated when the time is right for you, it helps make this experience more believable to the conscious mind that loves proof. For me it has reawakened a remembrance of a time before this earthly existence and given me a connection to my heritage. I don't understand the words consciously, but it's a feeling of knowing what is being communicated from my heart.

All of the longings I've felt for a family of love and way of life that is kind and conscious that seem like an ancient guidance, have led me to explore this amazingly advanced civilization. I have dedicated this space in my book to this lost civilization because I see the heritage of Lemuria as a way to make the shift possible for a planet, that by outside appearances, is so lost. For those of us who are interested and drawn to Lemuria there will be a reason. Accepting our Lemurian heritage, or any other, is not just a journey back in time, it's an awakening to the cosmic consciousness that resides within us. This awakening invites us to reconnect to our deep spiritual alignment to the earth, the stars and our connection to all living beings.

What used to be called junk DNA because science didn't know its value or understand it, now has new meaning. What we were told was that our DNA controlled everything, we were at its mercy. Thank goodness that was a long time ago and we are more educated now. Parts of our DNA are being turned on and off primarily by vibration. It's our thoughts and emotions more than what we eat or even our environment that switches them on and off. You have been turning parts of your DNA on and off all of your life without being aware of it.

In Lemuria we didn't talk about the chemical molecules that are stored in each cell of our body, we referred to it as your codes or potential that you bought with you into this lifetime. When you go on a holiday you plan and pack the things you think you will need for where you are going. Regardless of the planning you will pack things you don't use. Maybe the weather is different, wet weather clothes don't get used or you won't need that formal dress as it's more casual than you realised. DNA is what you pack for your lifetime.

Your higher self creates a plan for your lifetime. Before you arrive here, you know where you're going, when you're going to arrive, what family you're going to be born into. You plan and pack, your DNA is what you choose to take with you for the lifetime ahead, based on what you think you might want to do. You'll always bring more DNA than you need, and this is where I will expand this beyond the physical DNA.

We inherit physical DNA, (according to my education) twenty-three pairs of chromosomes from each parent, you become the unique marriage of those two sets of chromosomes and that's your physical DNA. Part of your plan or packing ritual for this lifetime is to bring a bunch of non-physical DNAs with you.

So, you have two physical strands of DNA with you, the complex double helix molecule that makes up your physical DNA and you also have non physical strands of DNA. Some research (please do your own) refers to this as the twenty-fourth pair of chromosomes and say ours will be activated as we make the shift. This is potential you bought with you, it may not necessarily all be used, but you brought what you thought you might need.

If you have a connection with Lemuria, it is highly likely you had a lifetime or lifetimes there. If you do, you absolutely packed some non-physical DNA because this is a magical time in human evolution, and you wanted to be prepared. In Lemuria we were highly vibrating, telepathic and heart centred beings, it was a society based on love. They were off the chart with what we consider to be awakened, psychic or clairvoyant, we had all the abilities needed for the 5D lifetimes.

We knew what it was like to live in that higher dimension, with those higher frequencies, and we knew what it was like to live in a society based on love. So, coming into this lifetime we would pack some of that potential, knowing that this is such a significant time, and we wanted to bring some of that wisdom with us.

Those of us with Lemurian heritage have Lemurian DNA potential within every cell of our body and without realising it, have been turning it on and off throughout this lifetime. Especially if you are on a consciously spiritual path, interested in spiritual subjects or the word Lemuria triggered something within you. Perhaps reading this book sparks a remembrance.

If you are consciously experiencing metaphysical happenings or information, this journey would cause you to turn on part of both the physical and non-physical DNA. Once you recognise that you have Lemurian wisdom within you, you can start consciously working with it. That's the good news, that's one of the reasons you've found yourself reading this book, to be aware of this.

Think about the abilities, the capabilities and wisdom that you have gathered during your different lifetimes- Lemurian, Atlantian or some other place. Whether that was for healing, shape shifting, flying, interacting with crystals, growing medicinal plants, knowing of our oneness, or whatever you can imagine, or remember from that time. You have bought a lot of that potential with you in this lifetime.

One of the indicators that you are awakening this non-physical DNA within you, is as you grow and learn spiritually, you become less and less dependent on getting information from outside of yourself. Whether that is in the form of gurus, books, courses, podcasts, or something similar. These tools are a great stepping stone, but as you awaken these hidden aspects of yourself, you will feel more comfortable accessing your own non-physical DNA. You will feel more comfortable accessing the wisdom and knowledge that you bought with you, which is your higher self. For example, you won't need someone to tell you that you had a life or lifetimes in Lemuria or Atlantis, you will trust your inner knowing. This is coming forward for me in some of the writing of this book.

You may have other indicators that help you recognise that in your own journey you are beginning to trust more fully in your heart and higher self. It becomes a very exciting way to live. I still enjoy getting confirmation from others or through synchronicities, that I'm on track. The more I notice these events the more often they occur. It's affirming to know that you are seeing signs of yourself becoming a sovereign being. That you can trust in your own light, your own wisdom from myriad of lifetimes you've experienced, in all sorts of situations and places.

For those of us who have this non-physical DNA, whether it be Lemurian or some other type, it is here, you can communicate with it and ask it to show you what you packed for this awesome human experience.

The ascension is a process that the earth and her people are going through together. The genetics of these people have been passed on to us, we are carrying our ancestor's history in our cells, and with dedication, we can begin to remember.

I feel like many of us first wavers had lifetimes in Lemuria. I certainly have some memories of this wonderful time. They were of love, community, belonging, connection to nature, and beauty so much beauty. It really was living in heaven, on earth. It's an experience of love that I carry with me, and it's led my heart in search for it. It seems to me we were experiencing a golden age back in Lemuria, so through the hundreds of thousands of years we wouldn't forget how precious it is to live this way, and to more fully understand what it takes to maintain it.

As I connect more deeply to my heritage, I remember feeling an immensely deep love for what feels like a soul family. Once we experience this, we never forget it. I was loved unconditionally by them, for all of who I am, as I did them. That was just the way things were, we loved everyone and everything, even a pearl or bird had as much value as a person. There was no greater or lesser. Not all, but many of the relationships I've shared in this lifetime feel shallow and conditional in comparison. It's a bit like being spoilt with unconditional love and then trying to settle for less. I still long to be with them and am beginning to sense my consciousness is calling them to me. As I continue on this ascension path, I trust we will reunite. I believe this with every aspect of my being.

We don't always know why the time is right for an event to occur. It would seem to be a reason connected to the bigger picture of life and the universe, bigger than what we are usually aware of.

The blessing for us all is that now is the right time, and the ascension process has begun. I'm sure you are noticing a stirring of what we have been conditioned to accept, all over the world. In order for change to be introduced and accepted, the old has to be recognised as outdated, heartless, cruel, redundant, no longer something we resonate with or have any use for. This occurs as we raise our vibration.

Our lives have been orchestrated by thinking, largely due to the patriarchal dominance over the last five or six thousand years. We have been taught since we were children to think problems through, to think about what we want, think about what to do, even to think about how we feel. This has disconnected us from our heart.

The main instruction from many homes, schools, universities, workplaces and more is that thinking is the answer to our problems. Thinking is as limited as the conscious mind, also known as our thinking mind. It is a thinking machine uncapable of knowing why we feel, act or believe anything. It is unaware of our history and is very much about looking good and being self-focused. It's been a great servant in this 3D reality, it gives us a sense of our individual self and has taught us plenty. It's connected to our ego and absolutely loves to feel in control. It is that chatty little voice in our head, that tells us what we should be doing, and that it has all the answers to everything. The truth of the human being is we are unlimited, so this tells us something about limiting our choice of self-direction to thoughts as our means of facing and resolving life's challenges.

On the way to this shift in consciousness, one of the blessings we experience is that we return to our innate wisdom of trusting in our feelings over our thoughts. Feelings have been negated to a similar degree to the value and respect of the feminine aspect in each of us.

This includes the running of our societies, governments, corporations, education sectors, environmental bodies, health institutions, financial institutions, business sectors, relationships and learning institutions.

Feelings are a part of our feminine aspect; they are communication from the soul. They are a guidance system from our wisest self, often referred to as our higher self. Which is an example of how important being in touch with our feminine side really is.

If we devalue them, we do it at our own peril, and as a result usually feel lost or like a boat without a rudder.

When I look around the planet this explains a lot. This can lead to you feeling depressed. Depression can be the consequence of suppressed emotions. That's how valuable they are.

We can make up any thought we choose to think in our head, but we cannot make up a feeling. Its either there or its not. If you doubt this, try to make yourself feel in-love with the next person you walk past or to make yourself feel such generosity that you want to give your car away to someone who has less than you.

A feeling is not controlled by the conscious mind. Feelings are information about us and our environment, whereas thoughts and beliefs are generally limited to time. Feelings let us know such things as whether to stay, proceed or leave a situation without knowing anything about it consciously. Our thoughts tell us the details past, present and possible future.

All feelings and emotions are either based in love or fear. The fearful ones can only come through the mind. While loving feelings come from your heart, the connection to your higher-self. They are your timeless connection to all that is. We can only feel now, not tomorrow or last week, only here and now. Even feelings from the past can be felt in the present. This is one of the strengths of feeling, we can only experience them when we are consciously present in our life as it is.

We have been accustomed to shifting our thinking from the past to the future and this is usually done out of fear that we will make the same mistake again. From this fear we ruminate, which can lead to us feeling victimised rather than searching for the learning. This pattern of thinking is often fuelled by trauma or the need to be in control which is a fear-based response. It keeps us stuck in an event that has already passed. An example of this was experienced by a client of mine, she'd been exposed to several narcissistic relationships. Rather than embracing all that she could have learnt from these experiences, she decided that all partners were going to cause her pain and for this reason, she would remain single for the rest of her life. The choice we always have is to stay stuck and become a victim of the past or take responsibility for what we want to learn and move forward.

Everything we need is here, right now. Lasting peace can only be found by living in the present moment, where the only point of power exists. It takes courage to sit in the moments of your life without distraction. We can't change the past or the future by thinking about them. Now is the only time we can do anything, including feeling a feeling, letting it go and choosing to live consciously.

The mind is only limited by our own perceptions. Limited beliefs create limited perceptions and affect what we make life mean. Our consciousness level is connected to the creative power of the universe, that is how we create our life. The mind is a powerful force that if misunderstood, can plunge us into the depths of misery or, when used wisely, take us to the heights of ecstasy.

As a Clinical Hypnotherapist my life has shown me without doubt that the mind is a creative instrument. What we think about, we bring about, what we focus on, magnifies. This is a living example of our God spark energy, that is creative in nature. The conscious human becomes conscious in the personal observation of this creative energy.

When we live unconsciously, we blame how we feel and what is happening to us and around us on outside experiences- our boss, our partner, our friends, our parents, the weather, past experiences, the planet or even God.

Blame is the unconscious escape from taking responsibility. With this way of thinking we become victims because we cannot control anyone else. Think about that for a moment, if the events and how we feel about them are happening because of someone else then we are trapped with no possible solution. The only solution is to take responsibility for letting go of what is causing us pain and this is made possible by finding a purpose. The result is attracting and creating the life we want to live.

Choosing to make this shift is doing the work of valuing yourself by letting love in. You do this by letting go of the pantomime of living. By this, I mean letting go of the notions that seem like you are living but you are really not. Letting go of the constructs that hold you down by opening your eyes and releasing yourself from the forebearers, tradition, the old ways that are meaningless to you and are without value. You do this by being true to yourself, authentically, honestly. It may be one of the most challenging things you ever do, facing all of yourself. Not just the light or the parts of yourself you accept and like but your shadow, the part you have hidden even from yourself. But how else will you know who you are? As you drop self-judgement it becomes easier to see the value in every part of yourself and acceptance allows you to truly love yourself.

This great flash or flashes of light that I will speak about in more detail in coming chapters, and I refer to as the solar flash, ignites the flame that is already within us all. This shift that is coming may be viewed as a disturbance and there will be some of that, but know this reality needs to be disturbed for change to occur.

We, as sovereign souls, agreed to this journey. We knew essentially what we signed up for before we incarnated. Regardless of what it looks like on the outside, while the clean-up occurs, it's all about saying yes.

Yes, to yourself to loving yourself, yes to yourself that you and your community have what you need to get

INCONVENIENT CONSCIOUSNESS

through this together. Yes, to surrendering the ego's control, and trusting in your innate knowing that everything will unfold as a part of the Divine plan. This, what is coming, is the reason for everything you have endured and everything you have been through.

Ask yourself when you don't know exactly where your heart is leading you, "does it make me feel alive?". You may be guided to jump into the unknown or a place that seems to buck the system and it may not even make sense to the conscious mind that is comfortable with being in control. There may be attachments, you're letting go of in order to take this path, those parts of you that want to grip on to the old. When we jump into the unknown abyss, it frees our energy to create the new with our ability to embody the creative powers of our soul-self. If a part time job that you don't love is necessary to pay the bills, no harm is done. You just want to stop doing the things that work against your happiness because your happiness is a gauge that keeps you aligned to your higher self. Feelings don't lie. Your innate birth right is to be happy. Follow your bliss, even if your ego bucks and complains, it will lead you home.

An unconscious life is a life where we hand over our responsibility to others and then blame them when it doesn't work out so well. It has been a recipe for disaster. Just look at the state of our world.

Therefore, it makes sense that a conscious life is one where we take responsibility for ourselves on every level. Know if something isn't working, it's up to you to make a change. This does not mean you are responsible for other people's dysfunctional or unhealthy behaviour towards us or others. Not at all. However, how you react to that behaviour is your responsibility.

Living consciously means choosing love, choosing actively to take responsibility for our own response to life by seeing the bigger picture of creation. It's knowing that every action and event is playing out for the highest good of us all, just as all of our trials and experiences have been for the betterment and growth of ourselves and others.

It's taking responsibility for our thoughts, words and actions. It means knowing that our perception of life is of our own making and what we choose to perceive will be how life is for us. Every time, without exception.

CHAPTER 1 QUESTIONS:

A) How would you define consciousness?

B) What do you choose to believe about the universe- "The universe is wise and compassionate" or something else?

C) How does that effect your perceptions, expectations and your life?

D) Do you think your human mind, body and spirit are capable of more than you have been told? If so, how?

E) What does your heart desire from your life?

F) Do you support the belief that all humans are inherently free? If so, how?

G) How connected are you to your feelings?

H) Do you have an intention to take something away from this chapter? What is that?

I) How will you know when you have achieved this intention?

CHAPTER 2

WHO IS THIS SHIFT FOR?

This shift is available to every person here on earth, the planet of free will. That is the uniqueness of our experience here, we have free will, unlike most of the universe. This almost guarantees that there will be those of us who choose to continue on this 3D path and that is absolutely their choice, there is only love and acceptance. There is a level of consciousness required to go with this shift, it cannot be bought, manipulated, forced or done by someone else. It can only be achieved by the individual.

In order to comprehend consciousness, it is valuable to look deeper into the meaning of life. Ask yourself: Are we here to just pay our bills, struggle to survive, spend more time at work than living our lives or with our loved ones? Perhaps if we are fortunate, we have a holiday once or maybe even twice a year. Is this all there is to life or could there possibly be more? I dare you to ask yourself the questions: Is this enough for me? Am I happy and fulfilled with this existence that I have to force and stress myself about day after day, in order to live in denial, fit into, or hide away from? Does this constructed and conditioned idea of living ignite my passion and bring me joy, freedom and abundance?

Living this current earthly existence requires you to be distracted by fears of survival, where you have to work on being motivated about life and all that it asks of you. It discourages us from questioning or thinking for ourselves. We are living an existence where 66% of adults are on some form of medication and between 50 and 97% of people, depending on their living environment, are sometimes or often self-medicating.

We are living in a world where one hundred thousand or 14.5% of people were proven to take their own life in the US two years ago. In Australia in 2022 it is documented that around nine people each day took their own life and that doesn't count for those that appear to be accidental. Up until now, this reality has been a life that we have to struggle and force to be a part of. Really, is this the best we can do? Is this the best our lives can be? It can seem quite depressing to face the facts, but this is what motivates us to make change.

To "know thyself", has been thought to be an ancient Greek aphorism. I take this to mean that knowledge begins with self-discovery. This is not separate from the fact that we are always changing and for this reason alone the path to self-discovery is eternal. We change our ideas, our thoughts and beliefs, our values, our self-acceptance, our appearance, our age and many, many other things in a lifetime. It seems to me that knowing ourselves is never complete but, on the other hand, we seem to have the opportunity to master ourselves in this changing environment. As a result, this mastery can find more permanence in our lives regardless of the changing exterior.

The idea that mastering the self is an on-going journey, is because our lives are filled with new experiences that call on us to master. We are asked to, and often ask ourselves to, master our thoughts, our emotions and our behaviours so that we give ourselves every chance to enjoy a healthy, enjoyable and functioning life. We can find mastery in the self or mastery in acceptance of how things are in our life in any given moment, often referred to as surrender then just around the corner comes another opportunity for growth.

This is an opportunity for us to deepen the concepts of acceptance and mastery, which asks of us to release the conscious mind or ego's need for control and learn to trust in the master plan for our life.

One of the major choices we have as we travel through our lives is: Do I put my head in the sand, go back to sleep and let someone else take over my life? Or do I step up, take responsibility and live a conscious life? It can be extremely inconvenient to choose conscious living, not only for us but for those around us who are choosing not to. But it will ultimately, and by design, lead you and everyone involved to your highest good and greatest joy.

Perhaps this is the result of the pebble in the pond effect. As we shift, we affect everything and everyone around us. This is a part of quantum physics also referred to as Collective Consciousness, as mentioned earlier. It's not always welcome because some people are in a state of resistance and want things to stay as they are. Even if, where they are, is painful and lonely because they feel a sense of comfort with the known, the familiar. Their eyes are not yet open. Knowledge of a grander plan and an honest desire for life, is inviting change and takes responsibility to own and an even greater responsibility to live.

When I make a change, things around me change, which is an example of the pebble in the pond effect. This can trigger people in resistance because change has occurred seemingly, beyond their control. The energy of their resistance takes effort to produce and can keep them stuck in the old ways, which to them feel comfortable and familiar, even if it means living in a nightmare. Their ego feels in control of what it knows and that is all it cares about. Most of us do this until we cannot tolerate it any longer.

The universe makes room for every experience, and one is not better than another, it is the individual's choice. On earth, we have free will and in the old 3D world, we are aligned to our ego personality. The ego cares about itself, how it looks and being in control. It too, like everything else, has served us well, to learn by experiencing what we don't want, which leads us to becoming clearer about what we do want. It's also given us a sense of self, a preciousness that is completely unique throughout the universe, the ability to know the individual that we are. It's our experiences that keep creation expanding, the self that we all are that grows with each new experience.

We are moving through an evolution of consciousness; it's new territory and we are trail blazers. There is no roadmap, it often feels like there is not even a path or rail. There is no clear path to follow because we are going through a vibrational shift while in a human body, for the very first time. We have to get comfortable with not having all the answers and sometimes not even the questions. Comfortable with not even knowing the path ahead or where its leading. We have to get comfortable surrendering to one step at a time.

It's a bit like using a navigation app. It's defined from A to B and can change slightly if you connect on a different day, depending on traffic or weather conditions but the destination will be the same. The difference with human evolution is the journey is not clearly defined from A to B, you and I are making this up, day by day. What is helpful is to know it's ok however we choose to do this, we can't mess it up.

The shift in human consciousness has already occurred, the destination is reaching a new reality individually and collectively. Our success is assured but how we get there is entirely up to us. The good news is we are always heading in the right direction, even if it doesn't seem that way.

Throughout the entire journey of humanity there has never been a more important time than now to evolve your relationship with yourself and with spirit. You choose what it is like for you to go through a fundamental shift in consciousness while being in human form. It all comes down to your relationship with the non-physical world. That person that you really want to be and that life that you long for already exists. *We are doing the work to raise our vibration to meet this life.*

The next stage of evolution as we create a more loving world is to align our personality self or ego to our soul. It is from this perspective that oneness can be experienced. As we make this shift, we will retain our experience of the individual self but it will now be connected to all that is, as we create from the energy of oneness and love. What I mean by this is: we will retain the memory of our individual expression of being this human that we are, while at the same time knowing we are connected to, and a part of, everything.

Hearing or learning something is vastly different from experiencing it. Experiencing something allows us to know it. When we experience the New Earth, we will also experience and know oneness once again, we will re-experience unconditional love and bliss. This creation is known as the 5th dimension.

Not everyone is comfortable with change, let alone conscious change, it often triggers fear. This can cause them to reject those of us who are doing this work because we symbolise change to them. This is the perfection of the universe because it calls on us to do the work to love ourselves beyond the judgements and apparent rejections of even those we love deeply. *The shifts we are making within ourselves spill out into our lives.* We change, our energy changes, therefore things around us change. Our perceptions change, our self-esteem changes, our confidence to be authentic changes, we no longer tolerate power being held over us. These changes can motivate those in resistance to create dramas which either push us out of their lives, they choose to blame us for something, or they choose to leave our lives completely. It can be challenging and require a lot of letting go, especially when those that we love so deeply seem to choose a life without us or treat us with cruelty. That is the wrath of the ego, it would rather be right than happy.

In my own life, I've experienced this and have cried an ocean of tears in the letting go process, as I dove deeply into my feelings. In these shifts, I have let go of so many things: the life I thought I was going to have, the people I was going to share it with, the pain of not being seen as I am and the limited beliefs that attracted these experiences. This led me to genuinely valuing myself. I realised you can't make someone treat you with kindness, by giving them more of what they don't already appreciate. I had to own my worth. And what I discover as I traverse this path is every letting go, creates space. These things I let go of were the gifts I received from these difficult experiences. It made space for my authentic self to surface. I began to value myself without the need for accepting less than I want. I realised that I am not responsible for how others take me when I set boundaries for my wellbeing. There is nothing real about attachments or false identities, they belonged to the third dimensional way of life.

As challenging as it has been, it has been made a little lighter by knowing that this path is in everyone's best interest, regardless of my personal wants. That is the path of the heart. Not everyone is choosing to take this path to the Fifth Dimension at this time. It can be sad to let go of the old and familiar parts of our lives but only until we shift to another level of acceptance. These experiences have given me great courage and in time, will continue to serve me by making me stronger while preparing me for this new reality. The essence of this shift is: I have given myself the freedom to be my authentic self and know my true worth.

This separation consciousness is not due to differences in perception but through the judgement people place on these differences. By what they make them mean. The belief people hold in right and wrong and there only being one way, and that's their way. People can only change that for themselves. This shows up all over the world, wherever conflict occurs. We see it currently in our world within the wars, people killing each other and being willing to die themselves, to be right. Only a belief in separation would support such a behaviour.

Until a person has done the work to know that they are responsible for their own behaviours, feelings and happiness, this will continue to be played out. This is the Karmic path, where learning is usually done through pain.

As a first waver myself, many of us continue to trigger fear in people. It continues to call on my own courage and heart to manage the projections of judgement and to demonstrate without attachment the faith in each person, to find their own way to wholeness. It would seem to me that one of the natural laws of life is in motion: as we make a change, everything around us changes.

During this process we can feel all kinds of fear, grief, sadness even anxiety as we let go of what was, and allow life to unfold, leading us to our new life. It is here we discover the peace that comes from trusting in the universe and living from the heart.

For us to play the part of a conscious traveller, we are required to be grounded in our every action, where we intentionally make a choice and know of its value to the bigger picture of life. Living in this reality takes great dedication, humility, commitment, courage, self-belief, trust and responsibility. Be assured that this ascension, transformation is not just for the mystical few, it is available to everyone, and it can be chosen energetically and consciously.

To choose energetically is to live from the heart, you don't even need to understand the ascension process, your energy will draw you to it. What does it mean to choose to live consciously or to wake up? Staying asleep seems like the easy option because it's just doing more of what we have been doing, and we know that road very well.

Following the old paradigm of making personal comfort more important than the true well-being of ourselves and the world. Consciousness is love in action and your heart will show you the way.

The truth about this same old road is that its destination is becoming less and less appealing even to those still sleeping. It is becoming so repetitive that we are even re-experiencing war, just to be really clear this way of living is not the answer.

Unfortunately, history has shown humans learn by making mistakes. Or do they? Does it have to get so ugly, and do the scenes we witness need to be so heartbreaking, the pain and suffering so devastating, that this shakes us awake? For some people, I think this is how it will happen, their hearts will be broken open. The struggle they experience will be of such magnitude that the only way through is to come together, which helps remind them of who they really are.

The particular process of this work that you are drawn to (and there are as many as you can imagine), will assist you to remember your true nature. In becoming conscious, you are shown how to access your courage to surrender and walk gracefully through the life in front of you. It ultimately depends on the level of resistance or surrender you are allowing in your experience as to how difficult you make it.

An example of this resistance to change is of a couple I know who were totally focused on making money and used substances and the high life to avoid themselves, their own suffering and their growth. Things in their relationship that were not working were opportunities that their life was offering them to grow. Then, without any warning, an illness struck the man, and their lives were totally changed. Many of the distractions were taken away and in order to find peace, they had to find acceptance in the life they now lived.

They could have stayed stuck in victimisation; we always have choice, even the choice not to choose is still a choice. Everyone has their own way to evolve and of course the free will to choose when and how. This couple continued to choose substances to fill a void that they even refuse to acknowledge exists. As life happened and the universe weaved its magic, one of the people lost some of their physical abilities. The distractions of the past that they were no longer capable of doing, left a gap which they replaced by spending more time together. That allowed them the opportunity to see and address things that could improve their relationship, with each other but ultimately with themselves. We can always choose resistance to change or the courage to surrender to where our life is leading us. Our life is the result of these choices. Many of us, myself included, continue to choose

INCONVENIENT CONSCIOUSNESS

to let go and surrender to the path our life is taking us on. This happens as we surrender control and learn to trust that we are being guided to our highest good, every step of the way.

I am a work in progress and still come up against challenges, as all paths offer us. I am happy to share those as an example because they can serve as encouragement. I am writing this book because of this willingness to let go and let God guide my life. I have made this commitment to myself, to be the best of myself. I practice yoga and meditate most days, where I receive guidance from my spirit-guides, higher-selves and, more recently, from my divine counter-part and the Divine. All of these actions that I have made a priority take dedication. They bring me love, a sense of belonging, stability, direction and support but above all they raise and keep my vibration high.

I will share with you how this conscious reconnection with the Divine occurred for me. This particular meditation has been life changing, I realised in this conscious reuniting with the Divine, that my deepest sadness held its origins in my belief that "I was separate and alone, separate from him/her/they/them, the creator of all things, therefore from myself and all". Can you imagine my delight when I let that limited belief go? I ask the question I'd like you to consider: Could the seed of your sadness also lie in this conditioned and limited belief of being separate and disconnected?

During this extraordinary process as I felt this conscious reconnection, I released the remaining well of sadness from my heart to discover that I am loved more than I have ever felt or remembered in this or any earthly lifetime. It was an experience I will never forget. I then felt the connection to all of creation and the love that comes with this connection. I understood in this moment how our belief in separation has caused us to disconnect from love, from ourselves, from everything. The most profound part of this process was to feel how much I am loved and how much love I feel for everyone and everything. My inner guidance asked me to surrender to it, to allow it in and to let it flow to and from me. It was and is more life changing than any experience I can ever remember having.

In feeling the love that I am, it creates a shift in perception. It is an experience, so it allows us to know in our bodies, that we are love. In this process that I am going to explain to you in detail, the Divine took my hand and told me that he/she has felt the separation that I had experienced and the pain it caused me and was filled with joy with our conscious reunion. Like most parents, the Divine just want us to be happy.

Within my awareness there has been a knowing that we have always been one, but since this experience the connection is more physical and experiential, this knowledge has become a knowing. It's as if we are sharing each other's energy side by side and it feels like there's more depth to be explored in the future. As this ascension process unfolds in my experience of it, perhaps this will lead me/us to consciously feeling one with the Divine in every moment, more consciously than ever before.

I have moments of feeling and experiencing this oneness and its extraordinary. The best way I can summarise my experience is I have a feeling of being home. This doesn't mean challenges will no longer happen or that my growth has finished. It seems to me that our evolution is ongoing and I don't think we'd want it to be any other way. But now I feel supported and loved more than I can remember feeling on this earth plain. Yet, in a strange way and at the same time, it feels familiar and even inevitable in some way, as if a part of me knew this would happen. I now feel a new sense of belonging, safety and confidence.

The meditation guidance I received told me my life was taking another change in direction. I have many stories of how this willingness to surrender has led me to this place I am in today. It has not always been smooth or comfortable but there is an inner driver to keep going, regardless of the events. Not easy, but always worth it.

This awakening or shift in consciousness is the next level of human development. Life progresses whether our ego wants this or not, whether we resist it or not. Resistance just makes it more difficult and remember it can only come from the mind. Life begets change and growth; this is everywhere in the natural world. The leaves on the tree change colour and vibrancy and fall to the ground in autumn, the tree has a quiet time of stillness in winter. In the spring the leaves begin to bud and grow until they fill the tree with new growth and this process continues, for as long as the tree lives. A dead tree experiences nothing, no challenges, no change, no growth and has nothing to give.

If we choose to surrender to life, the challenges we experience and the pressure these struggles create, smooth off the rough edges. These are the inauthentic or the conditioned parts of us. This awakening process polishes us into brilliant diamonds. If we resist our life's path by closing our heart, we call for a harsher more forced way to change and often this is where life is required to break our heart open. The situation as it is, is that our soul and the planet are on a journey of evolution into a new dimension of reality, and you can choose to stay where you are physically and metaphorically or to get on board. You can choose to resist or surrender. You are the captain of your ship, and you can either choose to trust in the Divine or let life or your higher-self find a way, and it will, to narrow your options and guide you to make a choice for your highest good and that of everyone. Regardless of the amount of guidance you receive, freewill allows you to steer your own ship.

This evolution or shift into a higher dimension will not only affect us here on Earth but it will have ripple affects throughout the cosmos. This is an exponential shift and is energetic in nature. This higher vibration that the planet and her people are manifesting, ripples out into the cosmos and supports the entire universe. This is a beautiful example of our oneness.

Divine timing is orchestrated by the universe and supports the divine plan of creation. When it's time, it's time, and no human or ego can alter that. We do have choices as to when and how we evolve but the way of the natural world is always moving towards more expansion and greater joy. One of the reasons it is time is because we've endured enough pain to want something different, enough of us have heard the call or did we make the call? Either way, the ball is rolling, things are shifting, the old redundant systems are crumbling, more of us are waking up and the shift is in progress.

Even though there's still quite a lot of work to be done, we will, and are, together finding new ways of being. New ways of living that are in consideration of and care for, every single one of us. Please remember your thoughts carry energy. What are you putting your energy into creating?

CHAPTER 2 QUESTIONS:

A) What is your understanding in regards to who this shift is for?

B) How do you see the Fifth Dimension/ 5D differing from our current reality or Third Dimension/3D?

C) Are you making a conscious choice for this lifetime to stay where you are, doing the same old thing (which can seem like not choosing at all and is ok) or are you willing to commit to your and the planets evolution? How will you do this?

D) Can you think of a time in your life when your higher-self was offering you a change or showing you some part of your life that was working against your happiness? Did you resist or surrender? How did you do this?

E) How does this effect your immediate and future actions, knowing this?

F) Are the thoughts in your mind that you allow yourself to entertain, supporting the old world of fear or the new world of love?

G) Have you, or will you, make time in your life for personal growth?

H) Have you committed to finishing this book? Is there anything in the way of your intention? How can you ensure you'll complete the questions and finish the book?

LORINA

I) How well do you know yourself? What is something you have learnt recently that adds to your life?

J) Is there a practice, idea or activity that you know your soul is calling you towards? Can you expand on that?

CHAPTER 3

WHAT IS "THE GREAT AWAKENING"?

The true self, Christ consciousness, The Tao, The Higher-self, Soul, it doesn't matter what we call it, so, for now, let's call it "awareness". Connecting with this part of yourself is like awakening from a dream of the character in the play of your life. Through your characters you experience the world with all of the beauty and ugliness. This planet is an opportunity to experience duality: male/female, dark/light, right/wrong, high/low, good/evil, peace/war, positive/negative, black/white, here/there and it's all a part of the separation consciousness. To experience these opposites or polarities as we do here on earth, we come to know how both things that are opposite can exist at the same time. It is here we can experience being separate, while in our essence being one with all there is, which then allows us to experience a sense of ourselves individually. I feel drawn to expand on this because it can seem like a big concept to embrace. It must have great value for it to be the overall focus of our earthly experience. So, let's go a little deeper…

In order to know ourselves individually we must separate ourselves from the whole, and we have done this through our conditioning that we are separate from each other. When we experience darkness, it's very existence depends on the absence of light. Think about this for a moment. There is *no thing* called darkness. When there is an absence of light, we can experience darkness. Without us experiencing this 3D reality of separateness, we would not in this experience, know our oneness. *We can know our oneness without a sense of individuality because this is at the core of everything, but we cannot know our individuality without knowing the experience of separation from oneness.* This is the gift we receive on this earthly plane.

In the ascension process, we can experience our existence as unified at the same time as an individual. This concept becomes clearer as you experience the shifts, and keep in mind some things need to be experienced to be understood more fully and with more clarity.

We have been focusing on our individual character's sensations and appearances with such distraction. Clothing it, grooming it, worrying about grey hairs or age lines, learning what behaviour is acceptable for a character to be popular, presenting this character to the world, making our character comfortable, pain free and as happy as is possible in the circumstances we find ourselves. Now, the time has come for us to wake up and realise that *we are not the character*, this is simply a part of our vehicle to experience this adventure. Waking up is demonstrated by us beginning to question, what we have up until now been encouraged to go along with. This includes our enquiry into who we really are, considering such things as: in order to know I am a character, I must have an observer of this character. So there appears to be more aspects of this character than we have been aware of, as well as a much greater depth.

Waking up is not for the faint of heart, it can be quite confronting. Firstly, to honestly face yourself and, secondly, to really see the undisclosed agendas of main stream society. However, these things are holding us back from the life of our dreams and acknowledging them is the first step.

The process is done in this order because we are the microcosm of the macrocosm. Partly why so many have stayed asleep is because it seems that in the presence of denial everything will somehow be ok. But how can we address something that needs to change, if we don't admit it even exists?

Just as valuable as doing this work, is not going too far down the rabbit hole of what we don't want more of. What we give our energy to really matters. Remember we are creator sparks. The discovery of the underbelly of our planet can become a distraction from your path. Like anything that captures our focus, if you give your attention to the problem rather than the solution, you'll get more of the problem. Choosing to wake up means saying yes to seeing what is really happening, both within and on the outside of our lives. Then comes the challenge, of finding peace with that.

Rather than forcing the mind through non acceptance, allow the mind to become curious to other possibilities through knowing what isn't working. Ask yourself questions and sit with the answers. The truth will reveal itself to you, when you are ready. You will know the truth by how it feels, the body knows and keeps the score. When you have an experience or hear some news that doesn't sit right with you, stop and check-in with your body. If you feel any negative feelings, such as pain or anxiety or feel uncomfortable in any way, that is your red flag. Using your body's feelings as a gauge helps you to learn to trust in yourself and your feelings are a main aspect of your inner wisdom.

I am about to make a big statement. Generalising is not something I normally prescribe to, but I am going to make an exception here: Awakening is the answer to all of the world's problems. All of the world's problems stems from delusion of the mind: that I am this limited character that believes I am separate and alone.

Due to this delusion, I grasp for what I want. Craving and going after pleasure and avoiding pain. In the suffering of this egoic based reality the world becomes a reflection of that same egoic consciousness.

A large percentage of the population are five sensory humans. They experience sight, sound, taste, smell and touch. These senses give us a personal experience of life and, in this case, is what I refer to as egoic consciousness. When our inner world is focused on the self, its senses become our main driver. What we focus on magnifies, the personal world is a microcosm of the macrocosm, or the inner world reflects the outer world. This is how our planet becomes a reflection of that same ego consciousness.

This is a strong directive that I took into my own life: Stop being a victim and blaming the script that has been both co-created and laid out by you, some through contracts of agreement, inherited by society, parents/ancestor's, environmental and biological conditioning. New dimensions are opening up within our reality or within the experience of life and you can choose to stay put or to make the break.

This is not a path to reach a destination but rather a pathless path. A stepping away from illusion and towards exactly where you really are now and who you have always been. The sun is always shining with the same brightness, and our essential being is always beaming with peace and joy but it's been too easy to forget that this is our birth right and natural state. This natural way of being is dimmed with agitation and that characterises our thoughts and feelings, as well as what we are willing to accept. It is created by this limited character.

It is not the body that causes us pain, but the mind, and the good news is, it can be tamed. When we let go of the character which dwells only in the mind, the pushing, the conditioning, the desire for someone else to be responsible for our lives leaves, who is left is our true nature. Me. Just who I am. This process is not killing the ego, it has served us well, but the shift occurs as we allow it to align to our true nature.

We do this by aligning the personality with soul, bringing the separate parts of us together. This gives us a sense of freedom where we know our expansiveness but are also more intimately connected. When we know and live this connectedness, the world we live in, or our perception is expanded and healed.

Enlightenment is not about becoming awakened, it's the recognition that we are the light of pure knowing, whose nature is peace, joy and love. Who is always this, and always has been.

You can believe that awakening is something mystical and that something like Jesus visiting you or seeing angels is required, and question yourself critically if this doesn't occur. You can also struggle and ask why: even though I am so committed to waking up, to being whole, why am I still experiencing periods of darkness or pain? This awakening is a chapter of experiences and more about a journey than a destination. It requires patience, dedication and perseverance to discover that beneath the layers of conditioning, this journey can lead you to reclaim the magnificence of who you really are.

Rather than pushing away thoughts or the old programs, simply let go of the interest in the thoughts and decide what you want now.

You can then choose something that feels healthy and enjoyable to focus on, such as putting on your favourite piece of music, digging in the garden or exploring your artistic skills. Music is one of many creative mediums that can raise our vibration, evoke emotion, sooth, inspire and uplift. Creativity in all its forms can also be a great distractor from thoughts and the mind. Creativity uses a different part of the brain which as we evolve, develops conscious connection to the heart and evokes feelings. We cannot think and feel at the same time, so creativity is a transporter from the head to the heart. Knowing that fear only happens through the mind, the remedy is to return to the body, where the heart's wisdom will, if you allow it to, guide you to a magical and joyous existence.

Your thoughts and behaviours are your choice and when you become conscious of that, you choose which wolf you feed by the thoughts you choose to focus on.

Some thoughts seem to drift through the mind, some seem more personal but every one of them is only an offering. You either take it or let it pass by with the intention of taking responsibility for how you feel. A thought only has the power we give it.

In my own process, after I've fully felt and learnt from the experience- when an old, limited belief or thought comes up, I use this statement to myself, "That sounds like the old me, I don't do that anymore" and I simply shift my focus. Rather than pushing away, or negating the manipulative thoughts, as all manipulation is activity of the mind, I simply allow the mind to be. The unconscious is just checking you are safe and still want this change. As you awaken it becomes increasingly obvious when a thought is attached to a limited belief or if it's an old program or habit, that you are not giving your energy to anymore.

Some things, usually learnt behaviours, shift progressively and with hypnotherapy I've noticed some can change instantly. The reason the older behaviours happen progressively is that the old synapses are still active, and they keep asking you. "Are you sure you are safe with this change?". That's when a gentle answer to reassure your subconscious mind such as this, is useful: "That sounds like the old me, I don't do that anymore". Then you have space for a new deliberate thought. Old synapses fade away, (what we don't use, we lose) and the new ones get stronger. You can get curious from there and ask your mind: "I wonder how much better this can get?"

We spoke earlier of the five sensory humans, and I wanted to talk about another type, the multi-sensory human. I heard this term from one of my beautiful clients who told me, she heard it from author Gary Zukav, who has written many wonderful books. I'm writing this (without reading Gary's book) from my own guidance, through my understanding and feelings that tell me this concept explains some mysteries about myself and others, who seem to have extra senses. To me this is the next level of the human experience, and it seems to fit the gap of where we have been as a race and where we are heading. There is a very high chance that most people reading this book are multi-sensory humans. Let me explain:

There are many human skills and abilities connected to and supported by awakening and I want to elaborate on the senses. Most of us have the five senses as you are no doubt aware but at this time it seems a smaller percentage of humans, are multi-sensory. My sense is this applies to the highly sensitive people. I'm not sure what that percentage is exactly but if Elaine Aron Ph.D. the author of "Highly Sensitive People" is correct in her research, she says they make up approximately fifteen to twenty percent of the population. I'd guesstimate that this is a rough gauge of how many of us are multi-sensory. If you have more information to offer, please post it on our sharing platform.

As I am one of these people both highly sensitive and multi-sensory, I will talk from my own experience. Yes, I have sight, I can hear, taste, smell and feel but that's not all. I also have other awareness's or senses. I know things, as many of my highly sensitive clients do, and these knowing's have nothing to do with the five senses. For example, in my yoga class, I know the next move the teacher is going to lead us to do before she tells us. Just like many mums, I know when my kids need me and at times when someone is going to telephone me or are planning to make an appointment to see me because they come into my awareness. When I get a text message and my phone gives off a sound, I know without looking, who it's from. This seems to be that I'm using my intuition as well as clairvoyance. I also feel how other people feel, I feel it as if I was them and that's known as empathic and clairsentient, in fact we have access to all the "clair" abilities including claircognizance and clairaudience.

Like many of my clients, I am an Empath. It can be interesting to know there are two types of empaths: co-dependent or empowered. This difference makes all the difference. Empowered Empaths embody this energy by doing the work to stay in touch with their feelings and keep their heart open which can be extremely challenging because we feel so deeply. The second prerequisite of this ability is to know yourself, to take responsibility for your actions and allow others to do the same. The Co-dependent Empath is someone who has learnt they have extra abilities that others don't have. They tell them when they are in danger and they use that with the intention to save others, fix others, (not that we can ever fix another) and this gives them their sense of self-worth. There is nothing noble about putting someone else above yourself or to try to sacrifice your own boundaries or well-being to attempt to "save" someone else. It robs them of life's natural consequences and they stay stuck. It's good to help other people but not when it comes at the expense of your own well-being. Some covert narcissists think they are Empaths because of their sensitivity to criticism and shame. They are sensitive to their own feelings because they are the centre of their universe and think this makes them sensitive. This is reflecting their sensitivity in a direction that sounds much more acceptable. They may actually believe this but to be an Empath, you feel anxious around an anxious person and truly feel heartbroken around someone who is.

As is the case for an increasing number of people, I can hear spirit; my guides and others from the spiritual realms communicate with me, known as clairaudience. I have a gauge on the collective consciousness, and I don't listen to the news or social media, but I can feel an overall energy. I don't know what that's called but I know it's something other than the five senses. I can also hear the voices of deceased loved ones of my clients, when they wish to communicate to them via myself, offering support.

All of this is organic, some say divinely orchestrated and not something I consciously choose, or can turn on and off, unlike most of the other senses; we can choose not to hear, see, touch or feel something for example. I don't control any of it, its more about allowing it to happen. I can, at times, if I focus in this area, read people's bodies, and hear what they need: water, vitamins, that their blood pressure is low for example. I've heard that referred to as a Medical Intuitive or even Shamanic, but the name matters little to me. I'm sharing this to encourage you to begin noticing, just noticing, if you can identify any other sense. There may be other senses that us multi-sensory people experience and it's likely that they differ from person to person. I'd love to hear from you so we can gather more information about this.

If your mind is waiting for, or expecting, ascension into a new reality as a part of your awakening process, remember, some or any expectation is a mind activity. We don't manipulate or strive to change things and to arrive at a mystical reality. When we awaken the perfection of the world is revealed, directly as it is. That's why some of my writing is still in a gathering stage, I'm allowing space for things to unfold. Is it possible to choose to be here, in this moment unmediated by the seeking mind? Is it possible to be with this moment as it is? Imagine, allowing yourself to simply be. This action is more powerful than you might know, as this allows for the creative and wiser parts of you to engage and have permission to play along with those other parts who have up until now run the show.

All we really have to do is give up the preferences of the ego and its fixation on things. We categorise life as good and bad, right and wrong and we focus on things moving around, using or getting more stuff. All of this is activity of the mind and we are not the mind. Its purpose was not to lead us. In order to transcend this mind focused reality, as much as we have learnt from it, we need to create stillness, quietness to discover who we are underneath the character. Then we can discover that we can be the observer of the mind and this can only be accessed in stillness. When we say, "I am sick of myself," that presents a question. Is there more than one part of me? There is a me who "I am sick of" and a me who is "being sickened." We all have expressions like this because we innately know there is more to us than the thinker of our thoughts.

There is a me who "thinks a thought" and a me who "can take the time and awareness to observe that thought". Just like when I say, "thank you for sharing", to my mind when it dictates old patterns to me. I am acknowledging a part of me that is thinking a thought. We are not only the observer of our life but the creator and co-creator of it. We are magnificent, infinitely creative beings.

Our true nature is love, pure love for everything and everyone, even the things our ego has a different preference for or disagrees with. I find that interesting, how much importance we give our preferences, and the funny thing is they change constantly. As a child I didn't like the taste of tea or sweet chilli sauce but I enjoy them now. My preferences have changed and will no doubt continue to do so. I've noticed as I continue to shift, I give them less of my energy, seeing them as transient and just an option of experience.

Have you noticed your own egos preferences? I like this, I don't like that, this is better than that, I prefer hot weather to cold weather for example. From these preferences comes a feeling of obligation to favour one over another and make one right and one wrong. Once we become more aware of what ours are and how they don't have to define us, we can begin to see the value in all things.

Awakening could be summarised as waking up to the realisation that our true inner-self or the "I am of me", is the creator and awareness of this experience. This is often followed by the recognition of our true nature, which is love, unity and joy. When we awaken to this perspective the world no longer becomes a place where we seek happiness and fulfilment from outside of us. The outside of us becomes a reflection of the inner-self because the inner-self is made whole.

This changes our desires and in this new reality they are not there to satisfy the sense of lack or something missing that characterises the separate self. They are soul driven, rather than having desires for the little-self or egoic needs, they are naturally in everyone's best interest. Mine, yours, everyone's. They are desires that support the highest good of all.

You cannot experience any event in your life without a vibrational agreement and *you are* that vibrational agreement. What I mean is, you set and adjust this vibration through your intentions and your vibration effects everything. It is energy that goes into the world and attracts your experiences. Your awakening depends on this awareness. In awakened relationships we no longer seek another to fulfill the voids or needs of ourselves. Such a person has found their sense of happiness within themselves. We come together to expand the joy of who we already know ourselves to be.

We then seek another to share the experience of happiness that we already have and it relieves our partner of the pressure of providing a sense of happiness for a voracious, unsatisfied self. When one person in a couple is unfulfilled in their life and looks to the other partner to fill that void, this is an example of trying to fill an inner void with exterior activity. I know I've had relationships in the past where both of us were expecting the other to make each of us feel ok, because our partner will reflect where we are at. We designated that job to them and such was our unconsciousness that if they didn't make us feel better than we felt on our own then one of us would leave, and the relationship would end. This is both demanding on the partner and only ever a temporary fix. This void can never be filled by another, this is our personal work. Yes, boundaries around being respected and treated lovingly are healthy but expectations for someone else making us feel ok, is an unconscious relationship lacking responsibility for our own happiness.

Awakening is the end of the nightmare and stepping into the dream.

There is no way out except through facing yourself and loving all of it. When you focus on the contrast, meaning the contrast of love which is fear, that's where your energy is going and it becomes your reality. It takes commitment to yourself to courageously abandon the nightmare about what we have been told about ourselves, about life, about God, about Creation, the universe and to step into the dream of our grandest notion: *That I am you and you are me, we are one and that love is all there is. That everything and everyone is a product of love, and this earth school is a journey of our own making to return to ourselves.*

To simplify our experiences into a model, let's say we all fit into one of three equally valuable levels of this adventure: The first group are not yet conscious, they are sleeping and learning in that playground. The second group are waking up and beginning to question and look at personal responsibility, they are exploring their wounding, open to growth and healing. The third group are awake and know their soul and light. They live from the truth of who they are, while still growing. This group are still doing work as the planet works in divine harmony with the collective. Many of us take on the collective wounds to transmute them but we trust in love to show us the way. This group is often in service to humanity in some form or another, cutting the path for others to move through while working through their own wounds. This service may be through a healing modality, the creative arts, writing, a mother, a friend or any other avenue available to them where someone is open to seeing more.

To be and know yourself as the light, you communicate who you are through unfiltered loving expression. The sense of who you are is portrayed evenly and fearlessly. The expression of love is an artful expression, your heart can become bigger, more pronounced, more expressive, more condoning of life and living. It can become more enveloping of all that you are seeing. Your heart becomes more expanded than is your current nature. You can hold more light, more endowment of grace by becoming more expressed as a loving being while opening your heart more fully to be loved and to feel love. The key I found is to hold no barrier between yourself and everything or anything else. Being loving towards yourself and others when you set a boundary for your wellbeing, can look like judgement but in fact it is the intension of self-respect and honesty that are aspects of love, that makes all the difference. *We are not responsible for how a person's wounds react to boundaries for our personal well-being.*

To be one with all things we must reveal our soft underbelly of our reflections.

You cannot hold yourself apart from anyone or anything and be love. You cannot hold yourself apart from anyone or anything and be love. You cannot hold yourself apart from anyone or anything and be love.

Love is boundless, it permeates all things, it must enter without reserve, enter freely for that is its nature. How you do this is to find the ways you filter your own perception and draw out these core elements of your own wounding. This can be described as "the meaning we give to things".

For example, I am going through a period of growth, learning to value myself at a deeper level. As a result, I have changed my approach to a friend who wants me to send time with her. Not ever to share fun but to listen to her same story that she's been repeating for twenty years. That nothing is changing for her, people don't appreciate her and she continues to feel unhappy about her life. I no longer go against my well-being with an intention to fix another. That was my old Co-dependant Empath's behaviour, "I don't do that anymore". Instead, I send my love and go to yoga or walk on the beach because it nourishes me. My friend can make that mean (the meaning she gives it) whatever her beliefs tell her. Perhaps that I don't love her, that she'll always be unhappy or something else that fits her perceptions. She can also make it mean that I still love her as I always have and I am allowing her to take responsibility herself for feeling ok. Nothing changes until we make a change.

The meaning we give events or our filter, reflects where we are at with our wound's and then it reflects our levels of compassion and how much we are embodying love in our lives. Through the understanding of these personal filters and as you heal, you can find freedom which allows you to equally perceive the hearts of all beings.

You are the only one responsible for how you take anything, or the meaning you give a given situation. Knowing this helps you to develop compassion for everyone because we all give life our personal meaning. This is often an unconscious behaviour until we become more conscious about what is happening. You can do this as you are working towards your own shift to wholeness, seeing yourself and life with more ease and grace, finding compassion for yourself. Viewing life with a broader perspective.

The unbound treasures of your heart are worth meeting, and, in this expression, you discover your heart needs no restraints. It can love all beings equally. It is through the heart we perceive, not through the senses of your own distinguishing abilities. Separation is the force that this knowledge provides, it separates things from one another. The heart joins things together, it blends and merges all.

The heart finds unity, the head finds separation. The heart unifies into love all that is expressed, no matter how it looks. This gives boundaries a new meaning, we still see and feel love but this includes our own well-being. Honesty is love. Not all behaviour looks like love, but at its essence brings about love. Even unhealthy behaviour teaches us to value and stand up for ourselves. It helps us evolve into a better version of ourselves, which is love. The heart perceives another being equally expressed and then your perception becomes unyielding, perceiving all things as love, including our reflection to assist in growth. Perception is love.

Most of us are not fully there yet but the shift occurs when you are living in this world but from a higher perspective, therefore, are not at the effect of its dramas in the same way. This comes about by healing your wounds and stepping into your own light so things of the fear-based reality, no longer stick to you or trigger you. Then you are without agenda, you treat others as you would like to be treated, you show genuine care which is not attached to a financial gain or personal agenda and live without judgement of yourself or others.

A valuable insight that came to me as I reflected on the many awakened souls that are well documented throughout history, is that there are many people in our current life today, who are living an awakened life. These are not famous people; they are like you and I just going about our lives while following our heart and choosing love. Every one of you and every group matters and is immensely valuable so wherever you are, whatever age you are, whatever circumstance: I want to say thank you and that I hope you know that you are not alone. That you are in fact a part of the army of light.

Most of us who are awake are still working through this shift as you can see in the collective or on the world stage. It is never our soul that chooses the negative events that are playing out in our lives, that is impossible. They are creations of the mind or ego self. We carry the energy of our collective experiences in our physical makeup, this is vibration and the only way to change our experience is to change our vibration. Every thought we think, every word we speak, and our every action effect this vibration.

The soul could never create an out of alignment experience, it is pure love. This is why we come equipped with our ego aspect, which is also pure love, as all things are, at their essence. Life itself seeks balance. All relationships demonstrate this; if one person is an over giver, the other one is an under giver. If a person in a partnership is so busy that they neglect their health, life can force them to stop through developing an illness. *The ego is the universal balance of the soul in this third dimension.* I think this puts it into perspective, rather than seeing it as the bad guy. It has played its role but like all things in the universe, it is evolving.

Many of us have made a commitment, a conscious choice, a vibrational agreement to live in alignment with our true nature, our God-consciousness. The timing of this differs for each soul and aligns with the collective shift. Some people awaken to these agreements early, some a little later. It can happen gradually, or seemingly you wake up one morning and the lights are on. The struggle is gone. Each soul has their own timing, and this supports us all.

Regardless, this process takes time. Old experiences energetically reside within us and can be triggered even from many lifetimes ago. This triggering event which most of us can relate to, is so over powering with emotion, it gets our full attention. There's no mistaking a trigger, it can make you stop in your tracks. It is perfectly designed to highlight where our vibration is out of alignment. Vibration always attracts it's like. Nothing happens without a vibrational agreement and knowing that, allows us to step into a new level of responsibility because we can recognise what is happening inside by what we are attracting. For example, you might attract a person who is treating you badly, when you are not treating yourself with the respect you deserve. This often calls you to set boundaries which is a shift into self-care.

I knew a woman a few years ago who was worried about getting cancer and would research it on the internet almost every day. It's all she focused on. She was healthy and played golf all the time but as you may have already guessed, she developed cancer. She used to say, "I just don't want it so I have to research it and know everything I can about it". Unfortunately for her, this focus as well as her mind set was the invitation.

It's the focus of our attention that creates the vibration. The unconscious mind doesn't understand negatives, so it creates whatever we focus on. For example, if you say, "I want to focus on; not having anxiety", because it negates the negative, the unconscious mind hears, "I want to focus on having anxiety" and it does. People say how can a baby get cancer but our body's carry our unique vibration from our past lives as well as this one. Our bodies can heal themselves, but we have to make the shift to believe that.

The more you focus on your soul and its belief, the more you are shifting your vibrational mix, to a higher level of consciousness. The doors start to open. The soul only knows alignment, well-being and love, so it sounds to me like a great place to focus.

You can build a relationship with your soul just as you can with activities and people in your life. We've all done this many times, so we do know how. The neural pathways in our mind are already established for building relationships. As you may already know, we create or strengthen these pathways mainly by spending time focusing on whatever we want to become more familiar with. I wonder how much time you have spent on knowing your soul?

These days I communicate with my higher-selves in meditation, and we have many of them. They reside in this dimension right through to the Twelfth Dimension and all of these are aspects of our soul. Knowing this, sheds some light on the extensive nature of our soul and how much there is to know. How can we intend to align our personality or our ego with our soul if we don't have a relationship with it? It's a bit like wanting to be an Olympic athlete in swimming without ever getting in the water and training.

Every chapter in this book can be elaborated on depending on the interest of the individual, these are an introduction to each subject. Because I've made a commitment to write, there are new things coming into my awareness almost daily. That is the magic of this journey, the synchronicities are astounding. It really is ever expanding. A playground of possibilities and adventures. Knowing your soul which is your pure essence, it exists without wounds and is perfect. It can lead you to knowing your true self and is the key to your awakening.

The famous quote by Aristotle, "knowing yourself is the beginning of all wisdom" speaks beautifully to this process. There is no way to fast track this relationship, there is a process, and this process could be defined by the word "Awakening".

This level of awareness is not just for the famous people mentioned earlier, we can all achieve this if we choose it. You may be awakened or on your way to that awakened state and, as I spoke about earlier, wherever you find yourself is perfect for your life's path.

That vibration or intention has drawn you to this book. People are waking up all around the world, perhaps your neighbour; the nurse who dressed your wound, the teacher who gave time in class, the mother or grandmother who does a lot or seemingly a little in the physical realm. As each person awakens, their energy or vibration has a positive effect on this world just by them being here. Abraham, a spiritual channel, who comes through Ester Hicks talks about the effects of awakened people living in alignment. She says how they are more effective than a million people who are not. That's an enormous result for doing the work to live your best life.

There is nothing more powerful than that; a human living their full potential. When we say things like, "my life is so busy, I really don't have the time to put into my personal growth", is there really anything else that you can do that can make you one million times more effective? Remember anyone of us can do this, it really is uncomplicated, and we can all get into alignment of awakening by focusing away from fear and towards love.

Choosing love consciously more and more of the time until that is your unconscious program; choosing love in every moment.

This choice of a vibrational shift will, in time, bring acceptance, kindness and compassion into every moment experienced in our society and in the world. It will be revolutionised by this simple understanding: *that we know that nothing happens without vibrational agreement.* We then know that we are that power, our being through its vibration creates our reality. All we have here are our intentions, our focus, our vibrational agreement and our experiences.

CHAPTER 3 QUESTIONS:

A) What do you understand "Awakening" to mean?

B) Who is this Awakening process available to?

C) What did you read as being a key or keys to this awakening process?

D) How would you define your vibration and your frequency?

E) What would you like it to be?

F) What do you notice about yourself or your life when you make a shift?

G) What is the value of triggers?

H) What is your sense of who you are?

I) What would you like it to be?

J) Do you have a relationship with your soul? Can you expand on that?

K) What does soul mean to you?

L) What is the power of intention about?

M) What is your intention for reading this book?

CHAPTER 4

LIFE HAPPENS FOR ME AND THROUGH ME, NOT TO ME.

There is nothing, not a single event that has occurred in my life that has not at some level bought me benefit. In the sense that every moment, every activity, every outcome moves me forward in the process of the evolution of my soul. As the title of this chapter says, and what I choose to think is "life happens for me and through me, not too me". That's why I came here to this physical realm; to evolve and of course for the joy of creation.

Let's talk about a couple of examples of this. 1) Over the last few days, I spent around twelve hours checking and making changes with this book. When it came time to send it to the type setter, I discovered it didn't save. The old me might have become annoyed with this. I did feel some confusion but sat down and went inward to discover what this was about. The messages I got was I was being shown how my personal shifts have helped me manage life with acceptance and that there were some other changes that I will pick up when I redo my work.

The second example- 2) My dear mum had just passed away which was a bit of shock at the time. She had a fall and her broken rib cut an artery, unbeknown to the doctors until it was too late. While respecting her wishes, passed on by my brother for minimum intervention, she bled to death. She was taking blood thinners at the time which seemed to add to the fatal situation. In time, the reading of my parents Will was in front of us, not something I knew anything about but was soon to learn.

In my birth family in order to be an executor of a will it was imperative that you were male. Even though my sister and I were the eldest two children we were told my brothers and brother-in-law as far as I know, were asked to be the executors.

There was never any question about that, it was just how things were. I was talking to my youngest brother just before the reading of the Will, who I was very close to all of my life. That may have been because we were more alike in our sensitivity and shared a more global view on life. He was talking about things that were in the Will, and I explained I didn't know anything about it. Probably because I was no longer married (to a male) so didn't have an Executor in my life to hear such things. He explained how my niece was being given a property but the other grand children were not given anything. I was a little shocked and expressed that it would be nice if the others received something, so they felt included. My brother said, "it's Mum and Dad's Will and that is what they have written, and we have to follow that." I agreed, even though to me, it seemed a little harsh on the other grandchildren. My brother went on to talk about what else was in the Will and I was listening but didn't really understand it all. I wasn't too concerned because it was what my parents want, so that's what I thought we would do.

The next week I was talking to a friend who told me I could and should get a copy of the Will so that I could read it for myself to be informed, which I thought was a good idea, so I did. When I read it, I was a little confused because as far as I could understand, it seemed to say something different to what my brother told me. The next time us siblings were together at my Mum and Dads house; I tried to bring this up but was told I just didn't understand it and I should get someone to help me.

After finding a local independent solicitor the story unfolded. I was told, the Will did not say what my brother thought, it said something different which was how I understood it. I let my siblings know what we discovered to ensure we were all on the same page. This was when things really amplified.

This revelation led to an ultimatum, where my sister who was the eldest of us four siblings called me for a talk. She said with absolute certainty, if I went down this track and didn't change the Will to what she and my brother's thought it should be, they would wipe me. I was saddened to hear that but also that my brothers were so willing to be led by this misinformation and need for control. This seemed to be asking me to go against what my Mum and Dad had instructed us to do, regardless of how I felt about it, which is asking me to keep the peace by doing what I was told. This had been a pattern of mine for as long as I can remember, to be a pleaser regardless of my own feelings. Whatever the reason they thought it should be different, didn't change what we had been presented with, and I had moved passed behaving in a way that others wanted me to. I had the courage to say through my actions, "I am me and must follow my heart, even if it means being pushed out of my family".

Whether we didn't agree with the Will or thought something else was intended or it was a mistake, to me, that wasn't what mattered. This is what my brother had said earlier and now things seemed to have changed. We had a Will from our parents and were instructed to follow it, if anyone had an issue with that then that was their work to resolve within themselves. Unless someone thought of an easier option, by making the person who didn't agree, the scapegoat. This is an interesting dynamic; the scapegoat is the person who is reluctant toward the abusive person's attempt to control them. They see through lies and deception. They speak up against injustice as they are very empathic. They refuse to be controlled and told what to do. I am a strong believer that everything happens for a reason, but this was testing me because I couldn't yet see the reason behind these events. But I knew how I felt.

This is the back story of an event that seemed devastating at the time, I had just lost my Mum and now my three siblings and their children were leaving my life too. However, I've heard it said that something happens to us when our last parent passes. It did for me at least. I began relying on myself and finally being true to myself, at a whole new level. I could no longer sit back and let someone else steer the ship of my life in order to feel like I belonged or was loved. I discovered this is not love and I was willing to be unpopular, finally.

When we speak up and feel the disapproval of others, it allows us to address our dysfunctional family conditioning and own limiting beliefs and self-worth issues. This is often why we don't speak up; it triggers the limited beliefs around rejection we have developed of ourselves. This is where courage comes into the equation, we have to be able to let go of the outcome in order to be true to ourselves. What I mean by that is, regardless of how my siblings responded to my decisions, this was how I chose to be and what I chose to do. It was my self-expression and it was an opportunity to stand strong and be ok with that. I had two options, to go with what seemed to me to be blackmail and pleasing others, my old pattern, or to stand in my truth. When our life teaches us humility over and over, we can think standing up for ourselves is arrogant or egotistical and it can seem harder to do. Regardless of all the hurdles, I chose to back myself.

As this event unfolded there was a deep knowing in my heart that "things happen for me, not to me" so I just leant into the grief and what felt like injustice, persecution, abandonment and lack of respect so I could release this hurt from my life. This has been the process I've used in my life many times to date, to uncover deeper truths and to step into my full empowerment. So, I just took it day by day.

This shift took a while, perhaps more than a couple of years until I was ready to find another meaning for this experience. I want to share with you what I received after I released the wound.

I knew this experience was no different to any other, it was happening through me, for my highest good. I trusted, in time, all will be revealed. I wasn't focused on blame or anger of being misjudged or even abandonment because I had felt those emotions and let them go. I realised that nothing others do is personal.

Things started to become clearer, because I was clearer. Firstly, I saw my family conditioning more clearly. I saw my limited belief that "people don't look after me". In the process I used to release this, I spontaneously went back into my younger life as a baby and child and saw how I developed this belief. It was connected to how I projectile vomited my feeds due to having a dairy intolerance and the messages I received growing up. I came to believe that this is how things are, and I learnt to accept it. Remembering our parents have their own unresolved wounds that usually effect their parenting skills. This belief and associated behaviour had set me up for this experience so that I would become aware of what my part in it was which is the only thing I can change.

LORINA

It almost feels like a crime to speak so honestly here, such has been my conditioning of hiding the truth about the dark side of life. Being conditioned to accept less than being valued and less than what I want. Even with all the therapeutic studies I've completed, I missed understanding what I was dealing with in this family dynamics, until recently. Mainly because I feel wired to see the good in people, but it was time to see more. Seeing more, usually coincides with releasing old patterns.

There are many dysfunctional traits and disorders that people develop for all number of reasons. One such trait is narcissism. I speak about this in a following chapter but want to take the opportunity here to use this experience as a living example. These people can show up in any area of your life, as they have mine. It's rare that we only come across one in our lifetime, but the good news is they are very predictable, and all have many of the same dysfunctional traits. They can be your parents, siblings, your children, people you work with, a person you are in an intimate relationship with, or an ex-spouse, friends, neighbours, anyone, anywhere. The penny can drop after the relationship has ended and you begin to put the pieces together as I did. The clearer you are about their behaviours, the easier it will be to identify them, and therefore set boundaries and look after yourself.

We can be treated with abuse, lied about, pushed out of our families, made the scapegoat, manipulated, controlled, gaslit, torn away from our children and grandchildren with lies and false narratives and be terribly traumatised by the people who project this trait. Still, it seems that naming it, takes enormous courage. My intention for sharing this experience is to highlight Narcissism, so that in may help you recognise these behaviours in people around you. Perhaps in people that you have been struggling with but didn't understand why. To know what you are dealing with is a helpful tool for recovery.

You can do your own research about the nature, nurture, discussion and many researchers report it's around 60%nature/40%nurture. They say if a child is raised by a parent without empathy, they can be more likely to follow this behaviour. There are some very helpful golden rules for narcissistic people, and these apply to all the different types which I elaborate on later.

The things I've found helpful, other than being aware of the type of narcissist you are dealing with is: don't engage them in conversation, don't go deep into anything, especially what you believe or think would be more functional, don't make their behaviour about yourself and don't expect them to change. These rules help us manage this behaviour although it is still very challenging. They will choose when and where and with who they project the more detrimental aspects of this behaviour, it often remains hidden from many people. The absence of real empathy means they don't care about anyone except themselves, and this can be hard to accept, especially as a sensitive person but it's also a necessary step to managing this relationship and healing from it.

Compassion was my answer initially, with the different narcissists in my life but in time I realised I was being their source of energetic supply, not to mention I was being emotionally abused. In many covert and obvious ways, this behaviour is abusive and can have lasting trauma that takes work to heal. Compassion doesn't mean giving in to what they want. Being abused is not a way to show empathy. We can have compassion for people and disengage from them. Otherwise, you are signing up to be a source of supply for your entire life, giving up on yourself.

After I became clear about what I was dealing with, I let go of my family patterns of giving and not expecting anything in return, and of pleasing everyone regardless of how depleted that left me. I realised it is ok to want respect, equity and equality in relationship, after all, that is what I give. I have found the courage to accept things as they are and let them be, just not around me. I decided, I hope they get the help they need but I am no longer going to be a part of this.

It's helpful to know, unless they know they are exposed and push you out of the relationship or group, there is no way where the narcissist is going to be ok with you leaving the relationship. You were their supply. *The courage it takes to leave behind what's not for you anymore is the same courage that will help you find your way to what is.*

Regardless of other people's behaviours, I was looking for the gift that this journey was offering me. It came into my life for a reason. In time, I began to see that if I cannot be who I am and have that valued in any relationship, and feel a reciprocation of giving and care, then it was not for me. I learnt to value myself and that is such a gift. I cannot be coerced, blackmailed or even convinced of something that goes against my inner guidance system, no matter the threat or consequences.

As time went by, these people remained absent, and my grief found a place. I began to notice the lack of drama and feel the peace in my life. I miss my earthly birth family, and I know they are not their behaviour, but I just send them love each time they come into my mind. I may still have some healing to do, but time will tell, and life will show me.

I have learnt so much from this experience and am grateful for that. They too have their own journey and I keep following my life's path, moving forward with faith in the bigger picture. When I look after myself my vibration rises and I am more of who I came here to be. There is nothing I put ahead of that. This is the greatest gift we can give humanity and the cosmos.

As my new path opened up, I've begun to notice new people coming into my life, and even strangers showing me kindness. I also noticed in contrast how much my clients value me. It has brought me to tears at times because I began to realise, I haven't had that from the people who are meant to be my people. As I raised my vibration with the personal shifts I was making, this behaviour and these people where no longer resonating and I had to step away.

Finally, I see this gem of truth- *You can't make people value and appreciate you by giving them more of what they already don't appreciate.* Finally, I got it. I raised my standards and began to realise, I am valuable, I am uniquely me. What I offer is valuable and I want to be included, cared about, appreciated and treated with respect. Giving goes two ways; we all need to receive as well as give. Stepping away from people or no longer feeling responsible for them, doesn't mean I don't love them. It simply means, I love and respect myself.

In the bigger picture of life, it was beginning to appear that the split between the dimensions was happening. Some people will choose to play out this 3D paradigm longer and some will move with the shift. *Not all storms come to disrupt your life, some come to clear your path.*

As time passes it becomes clear to me that there were several aspects to why this event happened for me. I have become much stronger, much more self-reliant and much more ok with being who I am, regardless of how others see that. What a gift that is. For this I am grateful. "It's not what happens", as the saying goes," it's what we do with it". I am deeply grateful to all the people who have created drama or separation in my life, they were a catalyst for change. I'm grateful to myself when I've spoken up and refuse to be treated badly, regardless of what that seemed to cost me. It was my path to reconnect with my true-self and my self-empowerment.

It appears to me we have soul agreements to help each other grow. What better way to do that?

We all have behaviours modelled to us as children and we can continue to mimic them or choose to grow up and find a way that is more authentic, less fear-based and more loving. I was a pleaser and very attached to what others thought of me but not now, that's another gift these experiences gave me.

My life has shown me how being true to myself is much more valuable than being included or being accepted by others that are conditional in their inclusion. It's not actually inclusion anyway, if you are not being yourself and are fitting into someone's fearful control issues of what would make them feel better. In this case, they are not including you, they are including someone they want you to be. This has built a solid foundation for my life moving forward.

How can we live as a sovereign being and do what we came here to do if we are looking for approval from outside of ourselves? The two things annihilate each other.

The first and most obvious way in which this event happened for me was that it helped me financially. Our family was not greatly wealthy, we are not the Packer's, (a wealthy Australian family) but what my parents left me helped me focus on my divine mission rather than survival. My path has led me mostly towards personal development and reclaiming who I came here to be, rather than material gain. But somehow, I've always trusted I would be looked after by the universe, that my physical needs will be taken care of, and they have been.

These are a couple of personal examples of "things happening for me, not to me". Can you see how the more recent event, "making changes in my book", was an example of being on the Dharmic path as I stayed in the moment to discover what the learning was. The next experience, "reading of the will," was still on the Karmic Path as this happened around five years ago and it triggered a number of past wounds. I think I'm transitioning onto the Dharmic path, maybe this is how it happens ... gradually.

Beyond the mind and senses, who are you? Who is aware of you? Many people think, "to know thyself "is to know the physical body but you are your inner self who stands at the centre of all your experiences. It's this self who is experiencing what we think and feel. Our thoughts arise on behalf of ourselves. Whatever activity or relationship we are engaged in, we undertake these activities and relationships in service of ourselves.

Ourselves stand at the centre of our experience, so what could be more important than to know the nature of ourselves?

Therefore, would it be possible to know the true nature of anything else if not first knowing the true nature of that which knows it? Think about this for a moment. Perhaps you might even repeat it, out loud. This is why when we meet a person who has done little or no work on developing themselves, they will often misunderstand us. They don't know themselves so can't know you. You can only meet another to the degree you have met yourself. Can you think of a time when his has happened to you?

I'm sure you can but the key here is, how do you feel about it? Why do you respond the way you do, or give it that particular meaning? Most relationships are built on not being ok as a single person but when I'm with you, I feel ok. Most people give away their power to others in this example. We are all capable of making ourselves feel ok and this is largely the result of knowing ourselves. Once we know and live this, we attract a partner for the joy of it and to support each other following our divine path.

Just think about all the events that had to happen in order for you to be exactly where you are in this moment. Most people are pushing to get experiences in front of them, to match what they like so they feel ok, even temporarily. Our experiences are the result of our beliefs, history and science, and we can either blame the experience for not feeling good or change inside. Most relationships are based on getting life to be the way we want it to be and to feel better, not worse.

In my understanding of life all conflict is the result of limiting beliefs and wounded inner children. The good news is both can be changed but they must be owned. You cannot build a happy life by getting what you want and avoiding what you don't want, especially if you are relying on events or people to make you feel ok. I'll love you as long as you make me feel ok: that's a bargain, a condition and manipulation. You have a higher place inside you, your heart centre where you can live from. The lower chakras are based on yourself and survival, which has its place too but are not about love. You store energy when you go through an experience that you believe you cannot manage, and this energy creates a block or blockages and then you don't feel ok. This is the energy that creates triggers. It's a feeling of reliving something that the current event is reminding you of but that has not been acknowledged and let go of.

True love happens when you do the work. Removing the blockages allows your energy to rise to your higher heart centre. Acknowledging the wound or past hurt so then the block to love is removed, which is the cause of you not feeling ok. There is a journey to being in relationship without expectation. It requires you giving to yourself, valuing yourself and attracting that reflection. When those who have not yet awakened come along, yourself acceptance is reflected to them. Your state of being is self-respectful and when we are without judgement, can withdraw. Being selfless is being ok while holding your true worth as a knowing, there is no need trying to be fulfilled. You are in the moment without any blockages from the past with no preferences. This is when your energy rises to your higher centre, your heart, this way of being depends on nothing. A higher relationship has no need, it's all about: "I am worthy, I'm full of love, do you want some?"

Some misunderstandings of who we are can be insignificant or even funny, but some are quite alarming, especially when our intentions are judged completely incorrectly. All people view life from their own perspective, and nothing is personal unless you have an old experience being triggered that's blocking your flow to love.

To live like this all you have to do is remove the blockages. That's what I refer to as "doing the work". The Shakti or your chi/energy is always working to come up to higher centres to raise your vibration.

The reason we need to do this is because of what we have made our experiences mean; you are hurting yourself by replaying the unresolved past and the moment you stop storing those hurts from the past and own the current experiences of your life, you are free. When we deal with life in the moment there is no backlog, and your heart is open to feel love.

I can think of an example in my own life- I made my past experiences mean "life is unfair and injustice means I am unsafe." With this belief active, as soon as I saw injustice, I would push people away to protect myself from an event that has passed. This inhibited me from building intimate relationships. When you pull up to a traffic light and someone toots at you. Now we are only talking about maybe a second of your day, and you can let it change your whole mood maybe even you whole morning. Just because that hurt you stored a long time ago comes back; you feel it because this experience reminds you of that time. The unconscious mind doesn't have a reference for time, it just knows it happened, and this event is like the old one that caused you angst. Another choice is perhaps you shove it into another area of your body and create another block to deal with later on.

The highest spiritual commitment you can make to yourself is not to meditate daily or do yoga, or workshops and retreats. It's the commitment to let those things go and not to store anything ever again. It's to stop letting those things block you from the love that you are and the life you were born to live.

You are not a beggar, begging people to make you feel ok, you are in charge of your life, you are a creator, and you just need to remember that. We are not talking about memories, computers have memory, this is storing stuff inside of you like an event you experienced that you couldn't handle at the time, it keeps coming back so you can process it and let it go. It didn't pass all the way through you. It's a scar or wound calling you to get what you wanted to get, the learning from that experience by acknowledging it. Releasing the old and not storing any more is the key. Now you know how it works you can do it differently.

Your heart is not designed to be controlled by others. Love is a place inside of you that you can't bargain or think yourself into, it's not controllable. *Love gives not but itself, love takes not but itself for love is sufficient.* This is the evolved relationship I call spiritual love, that we give ourselves and those in our lives who are ready to receive it.

When we understand we can only see other people's true nature if we know our own, then it becomes an opportunity to be aware that not all people know themselves. Therefore, respond with as much love and clarity as you can, without blockages. This is possible. We all see life through our own lens or perception and who if not ourselves, creates this lens?

It can be valuable to remember, that any misunderstanding doesn't change who you are, and it doesn't make those who misunderstand you, an evil person. Would it be possible to know the true nature of anything else, if not first knowing the true nature of that which knows it? People who don't understand you, don't fully understand themselves. It's not personal.

Perception is your headset, and you are not bound to your current head set. You can rewrite the game, your life's script whenever you choose to. When each individual disidentifies from their conditioned character then they are no longer acting as an egoic entity, that brings about a transformation of the planet and creates a new earth: the Fifth Dimension.

This New World is the reality of unity, oneness and love and we are helping it come into being, by talking about it. I've heard it explained as a dimension of spirit, we attempted this shift in the past but the difference this time is we are experiencing it physically. There is still an experience of I as an individual, that we have known up until now, while simultaneously knowing unity and oneness. Here, there is no fear and no illusion of separation or limitation, it truly is Heaven on Earth.

We have talked about Awakening and Consciousness and I will elaborate on what I'm referring to here as the Fifth Dimension further, in chapter six. For now, I'd like to pose a question: Could living consciously become mainstream in our lifetime? I believe it absolutely could, when enough of us make this choice. This is dependent on how many people awaken, on what is referred to as "Critical Mass" and it's coming ever closer. As I write these words, I know this shift has already occurred in the timelessness of the universe, but this information is some of the how it comes into being.

When enough people wake up, their vibration will shift this planet. That's how valuable your vibration is. When we wake-up we can see that very little, if anything, of the old fear-based, Third Dimensional energy is working. Not our education system, nor our governments, our banking systems, our health systems, many large corporations and companies, the environment/weather, our relationships, nor our connection to ourselves, each other or the spiritual realms. Many of the systems on our planet both internally and externally are ready for change because the planet and ourselves are changing, becoming more unified and loving. Those old fear based systems resonate with the old energy and have become redundant. *The pain of staying the same must become greater than the fear or pain of change.* And in many areas of life this is occurring.

This process of change has already begun and some of these old systems will be updated, and some will just crumble away to make way for the new.

Our personal work is largely about releasing old fear-based patterns that have had us living in an almost permanent state of fear/stress and dis-ease. In order to change this, we have to become familiar with regulating our nervous system so we can learn new behaviours. The work is actually quite gentle but naturally things will come up. This is essential to gain our attention and to guide us in the direction of our healing.

The good news is you don't need to walk through fire or have a huge release to signal you are letting go or making a shift. You will simply notice over time that you have a greater capacity to be with your discomfort and that how you react to situations at work, home or socially changes for the better. You will begin to swap being triggered by life's events because you are free to be present in your life without the past coming in and playing havoc with your emotions.

The problems in our world today are not political, not environmental or economical, they are not social problems. We are dealing with a spiritual problem. It's to do with how committed we are to stepping into a higher spiritual truth. This is not new age philosophy although it may be difficult for some people to hear; in truth these ideas have been around for thousands of years. Awareness has always been hidden in plain view. The time has come to stand up and say, "truly, we can do better, better for our children, better for our planet and better for the future of our world".

I have heard through spiritual circles and channelled information from Spirit, that in order for the shift to fully occur on earth the number of people awakened, or the critical mass number required is thirty-three percent, and currently it sits around twenty-three to twenty-five percent. I find this very encouraging.

I ask myself most days: how can I be more of who I am? Is there something you can do to add to this shift? Writing this book is my answer, currently. Peace and happiness that we all long for above everything else can never be found in objective experience or relationships, we have exhausted this path for eons of time. Understanding this clearly and not spending the rest of our life seeking fulfilment where it cannot be found, is breaking free of the conditioned programs that have kept us bound. Then courageously walking the talk of consciousness. We can then spend our time exploring this investigation into our true nature. It is the most valuable investigation we can make, on which our true and lasting happiness depends.

Don't look for an answer with the mind, let everything be exactly as it is. All negative thought and all negative emotions begin and come through the mind. Ask who is it that is aware of feelings or thoughts that come up? Who is aware of it all? Who is this essence of myself? As I explore this and put my energy here, it brings with it clarity and direction. Consciousness is the ultimate reality of the universe.

All sentient beings are localisation of infinite consciousness from whose perspective will view their own activity as the outside world. What appears to us as a world made of matter, our localised perspective from the point of view of our reality, is simply the activity of one infinite consciousness.

That seems more difficult to understand than it actually is. Everything is a part of the whole; it only appears different due to our perception. The ultimate analysis is there are no independently existing things. There is one independently existing whole. The unity of being only appears to be many things by the one who looks at it, which is perception of the infinite mind.

When we can see this, then the tendency of ego to take for the self falls away and we know again the truth, that we are all one.

I am the author of everything I perceive in space and time, being the ultimate responsibility. With this as my reality I am empowered to direct my life. This allows for peace to be my most common experience. Feeling and peace allows for flow and flow is the absence of struggle and negative emotion. Negative emotion is the result of resistance, we cannot experience negative emotion without resistance to what is happening in our life.

Flow being the opposite of resistance, must therefore be the result of surrender and create positive emotions. Is this not the holy grail?

"Life happens for me and through me, not to me" is not my idea but rather a statement that I heard somewhere along the path of my life. It helps keep me on track by reminding me that at all times and in all ways, I am being guided through the path of least resistance and to the path of my greatest joy. In order to take this path, we must surrender the often-addictive path of struggle. The majority of that struggle is the result of having been sold a lot of lies about who we are, what our body is capable of and the truth of our very existence.

What I have found to be the way of things is, the more we take responsibility for all aspects of our lives, the more freedom we experience.

By allowing others to dictate our lives and tell us what is right for us, we abandon ourselves and become enslaved and dependant. This truly is living a fear-based life, where this dependency steals our innate freedom and confidence to believe in ourselves and to be independent and sovereign beings. We are remembering the truth, that we are creator sparks and can steer our own ship with the guidance of our higher-self.

When we believe the limited stories or hand over responsibility for aspects of our lives to governments, family members or even a person supplying us with addictive substances, we become disempowered victims.

We can be enticed to do this with strong or manipulative personalities, even an employer who only cares about profit for themselves. This dependency steals our independence and allows our motivation for governing our own life to be diminished, at the very least. When we buy into the story that we need someone to think for us or look after us, whether its physically, financially or emotionally, we then become disempowered and enslaved.

Rather than believing that "life happens for me", we have been encouraged through the media, family conditioning and in our general education to believe that "life happens to me". This has been the earth story for many thousands of years.

The media news, if you expose yourself to that is full of it, *blame, victimization and misfortune.* We call it bad luck, or misfortune and have been conditioned to blame and see these things as a mistake when life goes so called, "off track". This is a statement of victimhood because in truth we are the creators of our perceptions of our lives, we are responsible for what we are focusing on and where our energy is being directed. The truth is, challenge has been a way to grow, not something to fix. Nothing can happen without vibrational agreement.

The mind is a creative instrument, and it creates through our focus. We even have the choice to reject this, which demonstrates the level of our freedom of choice. We can choose to stay in victim consciousness or evolve into empowerment. A victim needs a rescuer and there are many who are happy to take on that role but be clear about this: it comes at a price. If you choose to sell out, to resist taking responsibility for your life then someone else will. It comes with strings attached too and is in every instance an absolutely disempowering road. Neither road is an easy road but who said life was supposed to be easy? One leads to dependency, fear and slavery, while the other leads to freedom, peace and empowerment. Which way you go is yours to choose at any given time.

Those of us who choose to accept life and take responsibility have transcended victim consciousness and living life in an awakened state that offers adventure and empowerment.

If I could offer one gem of wisdom for your personal empowerment at this time, here it is; *Human consciousness can affect matter.* Whatever you look at consistently or focus your attention towards; (the past for example) will manifest in your life. You are that powerful!

CHAPTER 4 QUESTIONS:

A) Do you believe that life happens for you or to you? How does it do that?

B) Does understanding narcissistic behaviour help you in any way? How does it do that?

C) What do you consider "living consciously" to mean?

D) What are the areas of your life where you feel empowered?

E) Which area would you like to feel more empowered?

F) What are you prepared to do to achieve this?

G) Do you think the systems of our planet are all functional or that some of them are largely redundant and in need of change? If so, what changes would you like to see?

H) Do you prefer to keep things as they are on our planet, for comfort of the familiar or are you ready for change? Explain why you feel this way?

I) What changes would you like to see?

J) What is your personal story (the story you tell yourself) of what you are responsible for and capable of?

K) What would you like to change and what would you like to remain the same in this story?

CHAPTER 5

SENSITIVE PEOPLE ARE THE FROGS OF OUR PLANET

Healthy frog populations are generally a good indication of a healthy environment. Most common frogs live in and around fresh water. While they are usually small and often go unseen, frogs are also an essential thread in the food web. Frogs eat vast amounts of invertebrates, including houseflies, mosquitoes, cockroaches and spiders and they are a fundamental food source for a wide variety of other wildlife including birds, mammals and reptiles. Tadpoles fill our creeks and dams, helping keep algae and mosquito larvae under control, while they too become food for fish and other wildlife.

Frog populations are declining around the world for a wide range of reasons, including habitat loss and disease. They are an obvious sign that the environment is unhealthy and in need of attention. The disconnection we have to ourselves, expands into the disconnection we have with nature. This is scientific information that we can all access and this last example more obviously connects them to us sensitive people. I say, "us" because as well as being a highly sensitive person myself, it's highly likely that many of my readers are sensitive people or you may know at least one in your own lives.

Frogs absorb oxygen and other compounds through their skin, making them sensitive to pesticides, herbicides and their environment in general. Nature expresses itself organically and without agenda. It is showing us what we often miss or don't wish to see.

Sensitive people can go by many names including empaths, highly sensitive people (HSP), Star-Seeds, Blue Ray Indigo Star-Seeds, Blue Ray Empaths, Indigos, and Rainbow Warriors (all easily researched). If you know of others, please share it in my blog. These people are all highly sensitive to their environment and have a deeper purpose for being here at this time of great need and change. I imagine that most of us, maybe all of us experience extreme heights of the feeling sense. We not only feel our own experiences very deeply but also those of others. This is both a challenging and extremely rewarding life that no one can consciously choose or un-choose. It is simply who we are. The choice comes when we decide to be co-dependant or empowered as a highly sensitive person.

Being a highly sensitive person myself, HSP, I will use the first-person plural pronoun "we' as I talk further about sensitive people. We feel "everything" deeply and a great deal more than the general population. It is at the moment, as far as I am aware, impossible to measure sensitivity in humans. Except I can say that I can feel their sensitivity and I want to say it's of a finer vibration than most. Through personal observation of the general reactions of those HSP people around me and my own, it seems to me that we have increased sensitivity somewhere in the vicinity of a twenty-five to around eighty percent to the majority of the population. That heightened sensitivity involves all of our senses.

The majority of the population are unaware that a HSP is a real type of human, quite unique in many ways. This has gone unacknowledged for thousands of years, possibly because most of humanity has disconnected from their own sensitivity out of protection and fear of survival therefore, little is understood about the trait. We have been called "too sensitive", "over sensitive" and "high maintenance". In the healthcare system it hasn't been taken into consideration at all, nor in our education system, work places, families or in any aspect of society. It has gone unacknowledged for long enough.

Some of our unique differences are: we experience big feelings. We love very deeply. We take longer to heal from medical procedures. We are more adversely affected by pharmaceuticals and synthetic substances or most unconscious manmade products. We do well with products derived from nature and usually do better with natural remedies. When being prescribed medication, we usually require different doses to the mainstream population or people who are not HSP. We also know things about our bodies and other people, things that are not necessarily provable by measurements or sight.

We know when music is too loud and when the person we are talking to is anxious, even if they are unaware of it themselves. We typically learn by doing things rather than reading from a screen or white board. This is because we are kinaesthetic learners and when misunderstood are often judged as not smart, which is quite the opposite of the truth. There are many areas we can be misunderstood. We can even be misdiagnosed which can lead to life threatening outcomes because this phenomenon is rarely acknowledged or understood. Having said all of this, you can probably see why it's important to shift people's perception.

One of the challenging aspects of an empowered empathic highly sensitive person, is when we reflect back to others, their disowned or unresolved negative emotions and behaviours. Sometimes we say something we wouldn't normally say for example, and this can be triggering for others. This is done through our intension to serve others to transcend their shadow selves, however, this often triggers people's judgements, which they project onto us. As challenging as some aspects are, it is still the only way I want to be and every challenge, without exception, brings a gift. It is my passion, well one of them, to educate as many people as possible about HSP.

Native American's, have a prophecy which speaks to the purpose of these sensitive people or "Rainbow Warriors" as they are sometimes referred to: "When the earth is ravaged and the animals are dying, a new tribe of people shall come unto the earth from many classes and who by actions and deeds shall make the earth green again. They shall be known as the Rainbow Warriors." There are specific streams of wisdom held within their DNA and their high heart centre. Indigos and star seeds have been coming in for some time, it seems to me ever since the first wavers arrived.

I refer to this name "First wavers" from the work of Dolores Cannon, a famous past life clinical hypnotherapist who has now passed over. She talked about the three waves of volunteers who began to arrive back in the late fifties and early sixties. This information was received from her clients when in Hypnosis. She discovered not only can the human go back in time to a past life and to the source of creation, but they can go forward to a time far beyond our future. It became a way for her to research history, and she found knowledge that was lost, distorted or unknown.

Dolores was told that earth being a young planet, and with the possibility of self-destruction we needed some other souls to be brought in that were not stuck on the wheel of Karma. Perhaps that's what has made it possible for me, to step away from unconscious behaviour in my earthly family and step into my destiny, even though it has been heartbreaking.

These were the three waves of volunteers that came here to help earth because what we do here affects the entire cosmos and the behaviour here was extremely destructive.

Each wave has unique characteristics. The first who would be somewhere in their mid-sixties, early seventies now and are the warriors, as they cut the path for the others. They found it incredibly difficult to be here and many took their own life. They are known as "The keepers of the garden". They abhor violence; they arrived after the horrors of the Hiroshima bombing.

The second wave would be approximately in their late thirties or early forties currently. They are the generators and channels and do not usually have children. Their role is to simply be here, they affect everyone they are around with their energy. The third wave are known as, "The Hope of the World" and the Indigo Children, they are sensitive so do not do well in any environment that doesn't' recognise this. They don't respond well to pharmaceuticals, they get bored easily and love challenges. These waves of beings also speak to the Blue Ray's, Indigos, Star-Seeds, and Empaths as they came from all over the Cosmos.

Delores discovered we can access the unconscious mind and a deeper part of psyche. This she referred to as the Over-Soul, the Higher-Self, the Higher Consciousness. From here she gained other worldly insights. I talk with my clients loved ones' higher-selves on occasion, and it takes my breath away. How magnificent this aspect of us is. This is an experience engaging with the truth of us, the place of miracles and healing and it's completely loving.

This part of us can direct healing to our body, as that is how we are designed. If you are responsible for making yourself sick and you are, you can also heal yourself. You are that powerful. Your mind has a reason for doing everything. Its only intention is to help guide you to your best life. It's only the limited and faulty programs that we have been given that lead the mind astray.

I often use this example of the mind's positive intentions to my clients: The Japanese holdouts were soldiers from the Imperial army in the jungle on Lubang island near Luzon, in the Philippines. The communication had been cut off and they were honour bound never to surrender. When World War two ended in 1945 it was difficult to get the message to these soldiers. The initial attempt was, I believe, to drop leaflets from an aircraft on the beach. The soldier's read them and said, "this is the enemy trying to get us to leave. We are not leaving our post. We are honour bound and we will stay". The next attempt was to send in some natives. After learning the language which took some time, they were instructed to give the soldiers this news. They too attempted to pass on the message that the war was over, and again, the soldiers doubted the veracity of the message to surrender. Eventually in 1974 their aging former commanding officer was flown in to see them. Correspondents say, they were greeted as heroes on their return to Japan. They were the soldiers who held the ground. They stayed until they knew it was time to leave.

This is how the unconscious mind works. It decides on something that it believes will help you and will not change that until it knows you are safe without that behaviour. That's why you can know what a healthy diet is but still choose to eat lots of sugar. Other examples are: smoking, fear of flying, fear of abandonment, anxiety etc. The mind began these behaviours with the best of intent. This is when hypnosis is a wonderful tool for its ability to change the unconscious mind. It takes your willingness and self-awareness, as all change does but can be made much more efficient and effective with the help of hypnosis.

When you find out why you made yourself sick it will go away because you know the reason, and what your body was trying to tell you. You can do this any number of ways: by connecting to your higher-self in meditation, through Hypnotherapy, with the help of a book I recommend, "The secret language of the body" by Inna Segal, or any way that works for you. We just need to value ourselves for who we really are. Again, please do your own research here. If you're interested, Dolores Cannon has written many, many books.

I will dedicate a large section of this chapter to Blue Ray Star-Seeds as I am guided to do. It speaks to my own heritage and has helped me understand another part of who I am. For those unique humans that are a Blue Ray or Blue Ray Indigo and part of that cosmic lineage, re-awakening to the wisdom within you will happen in divine timing. You will find a way to bring that wisdom through with your unique expression and gifts. This is why tapping into your unique magic is the key. Our purpose as a warrior is love and protection, a guardianship role for humanity. The goal of many of these highly sensitive races and Star-Seeds is to assist humanity, including the consciousness we call Gaia, our planet earth. The reason is, this is a time of great need. It's the end of a long cycle; it's a time when humans get to choose what's next for their soul's construct.

In this realm there is an added layer of work to assist humanity and all living beings to break free of this false prison that was created by what could justly be called evil, non-benevolent beings that broke into this realm in ancient times. This may be challenging for some to believe, but waking up involves facing the darkness. How else can we address it?

LORINA

It's been a constant struggle to get underneath the falsity of this prison, this slavery existence, that these evil beings from other realms have created. The good thing to know is there are many beings from other realms sending assistance consistently. As we open our eyes, we begin to notice assistance in many different forms, some things that might be called miracles or a freak event. The ultimate goal is to offer serenity and freedom to souls that have a yearning to get out and break free from this false prison. The desire we have for freedom is our soul reminding us, this is not the way we were intended to live.

Lightworkers, or those who are here to help in the ascension of the planet through the use of their own unique healing abilities and speaking the truth, intend to free those who have been trapped in repeated re-incarnation cycles, with one of the biggest traps of all. The thing we have called Karma, which is just things we have been encouraged to believe that keep us stuck. Whatever you believe in, you create.

These Blue Rays and Star-Seeds are from varied guardian places, a higher original meaning that you might call creator realms. These are places that are far more advanced in knowing. They are positive vibrational realms. Each one of us are bringing through from higher dimensions, this unique ray to express in our way or magic. Listen to your knowing of these words, feel them as you too, can awaken to even a deeper level. I remember doing a process in the spiritual group I was in in the early 2000's and being told that I was carrying the ray of unconditional love. Through experience and learning, I now understand more about this. It appears that those people who have embraced unconditional love feel comfortable sharing my life. Those who haven't, struggle with the reflection I mirror.

As we embrace our true heritage, we will see a shift in the world around us. Similar to how we have begun to accept differing sexual preferences and identities, to alleviate the fear and judgement that often accompanies lack of understanding. But we must first understand ourselves.

It feels like I imagine coming out would be, when we own our sensitivity. My intention is to have it feel like something to be proud of, as we would any other aspect of our essence. Being highly sensitive is a well earnt expression of who we are. Many people fear their feelings and I see sensitivity as a courageous trait, it has resulted from lifetimes of facing our own pain and a deep caring for everything and everyone.

The fear of past persecution can kick the magic out of us, as many of us lightworker's experienced over many lifetimes. But we hold the key to our own freedom by boldly stepping into our creative outlets through our unique expression. The Blue Ray is connected to the throat chakra and the third eye, so that expression is usually about getting the magic out into the world through communication.

We, the sensitives are here to share our gifts, the persecution has continued even though that looks different today. We're still seeing it playing out. For example, we will see people not liking our social media posts, they may make comments while we are socialising, single us out so there will be some back lash in some way because the truth really does trigger people.

I have personally experienced modern-day persecution as many of us have. As we move through our shadows and begin to embrace more of our light this shift in our vibration can trigger people around us. I do at times, with my energy signature, reflect other people's unresolved negativity and it can trigger negative projections. It can feel strange to say something you wouldn't normally say or feel a negative emotion that you have already healed. This reflection is designed to bring into the light that which is being denied. I was still carrying a limited belief about being misunderstood and abandoned which is a part of the belief around persecution. We have to have the vibration that matches whatever we are attracting. The vibrational agreement, that magnetizes it to us.

When a person feels insecure around someone who is doing the work, it can show up as jealousy. This can lead them to cruel behaviours they wouldn't normally do. The example here is of a good-hearted woman I know who says she is an Empath and Sensitive. This is a great example of an empath living out of balance or a co-dependent empath. We can all do this, deny our darkness which only gives it more power. Assertiveness becomes aggression in this dynamic and this lack of alignment creates fear from which manipulation results. I have no doubt that this is all a part of the cleaning up and waking up that is required for us all to choose our path moving forward.

When people are living out of balance, life has a way of getting their attention. Sometimes through illness, so called accidents, relationship break downs or financial situations. If you look at your life you will see, the majority of your learnings have been through one of these three avenues- money, relationships or health. Mine is has certainly been relationships. We are all being given the opportunity to wake up and be the best version of ourselves.

As someone famous once said, "What we do to another, we do to ourselves". This is because we are one. These dysfunctional actions are persecution of today's kind. Regardless, I have love and feel compassion for these and all people because people are not their behaviour, and my life continually shows me, everything serves a purpose.

The path of a Blue Ray or any kind of sensitive person is not without its challenges. When we say yes and launch into our missions, we are stepping into our power fully, and honestly there is no other way to accomplish this journey. The heart of our mission is transmutation through alchemy. We will recognise our family Blue Rays by how they present similar information such as this book. We present this wake-up call and transmutation in our own unique ways. Writing, speaking, documentaries, movies, music, etc.

I am so excited for these reunions. At birth the Blue Ray's veil of who they are is thinner than most people's, even if we can't put it into words. We will use the platform we find ourselves in. I was brought up in the Catholic religion and I constantly had questions and knew that many things were "off", they just didn't make sense to me. Even though this was the case at that time, I still had a desire to be a nun. It seemed like the closest thing I knew of, that seemed to address this longing for connection to my spiritual self, which has always meant everything to me.

Sensitivity like most things, varies from one person to another. Dr. Elaine Aron in her book "The Highly Sensitive Person" explains how she has researched the population and concludes that fifteen to twenty percent of the population are highly sensitive. I often think about the sensitive people I've met; either in my career or socially and think what a different world we would live in if everyone was a balanced and empowered HSP. Due to the fact we know and feel our oneness, there would be none of today's struggles of war, poverty or isolation, and we would all experience a world of love, kindness and unity.

I have become aware more recently that many of the babies being born in the last ten years or so are highly sensitive people and this may not have been taken into consideration in books written prior to this time. To me this speaks to the shift that is occurring on our planet and how these souls are here to assist in their own unique ways. The powerful language we speak is emotion and it comes through as empathy. What I know is Blue Rays are wise in different ways; it's not mind wise. It's the wisdom that's held by speaking the language of emotion through empathy.

Empathy is soaked into our being through all centres and helps our minds to make all kinds of connections. We can see clearly what is wrong, where there's truth lacking, we can really see into the underbelly and underworld, incredibly easily. However, this information is not always welcomed, as some people prefer not to know, because the truth seems more than they can manage.

I am speaking more specifically about the Blue Rays because this is my area of personal understanding, and I trust a large portion of my readers are here to identify this or some sensitive trait within themselves. The healing that we Blue Rays are here to bring with our unique mastery is really about the energy of transmutation, this is alchemy. We are the Alchemists.

All humans have the capacity to be an Alchemist. Alchemy is about transmuting one emotion into another: sorrow into happiness, pain into action to heal that pain. *Blue Rays focus on that transmutation mastery as a speciality. We are here to transmute the deepest, the most unseen, underbelly aspects of what is going on in the 3D experience and it means we are going to deal with things that many others don't.* It's not easy, it's a huge undertaking being a warrior and guardian of the earth, of

Gaia. A guardian is about protecting and assisting so it's not glamorous, it's a choice to bring through our essence into human form. I find it develops strength and is a privilege.

We experience injustices, illness, family dysfunction, persecution and we are often given the role of scapegoat, because the energy we anchor into this reality transmutes and brings the horrific injustices and suffering, the underbelly of the planet, to the surface. We are transmuting that all through our body, through our energy field, which is why many of us spend time away from mainstream life. Many of us, if not all of us have periods of being a hermit. I certainly do.

Indigos, Blue Rays, Star-Seeds, Empaths and Light workers in general (those of us who are here to bring light to the planet) are naturally drawn to exposing the truth in this matrix. This book is largely about that. This is simply our soul's purpose and the intensity of our energy field because that's what the energy field is designed for. I used to think I was faulty because I felt a strong desire to expose the lies of this planet, but now, I understand why. I think many of us have felt this. It feels reassuring when we can make sense of our inner world.

As Lightworkers, our energy field often triggers unconscious behaviour or Karmic patterns in others and that happens just by the vibration we hold. It's not an easy thing to manage but our energy fields bring unconscious wounds to the surface of those people around us, and at times, these are projected onto us. We are the people that other people tell their deepest darkest secrets to. This is why the Blue Rays energy field are the only kind of energy field that can hold space for the profound level of what we call the unseen, the negative and the evil. We call the Indigo Blue Rays the holders of space. But we don't hold space to justify any of that suffering therefore we keep in mind the long-term wellbeing of ourselves and all. We have the capacity to hold and unlock the draconian timelines or negative 3D energies and bring to light ways to reconfigure human creation or the original human blueprint. This allows more positive frequency to anchor into this realm. We truly get rid of the old to awaken the new. I hope you can see how acknowledging this connects into the great awakening and shift.

This alchemical energy, whether you are a Blue Ray, Indigo, Star-Seed or some other type of sensitive person or Empath, can attract both narcissistic and gaslighting behaviours which can be extremely challenging to manage. I'd also like to highlight that all these pains are tools that assists us in building strength and guiding us towards letting go of what is not a part of our essence. These challenges call on our authentic selves to alchemise negative energy and hold our light strongly. It can never be underestimated that all of the pain and struggles you go through as a warrior of the light, whether it be in relationship, through wealth or health, all of it has brought you to where you are today.

As I clarify what these narcissistic and gaslighting traits look like, I want to make it clear that this information comes completely from my observations and life experiences. This is not meant to represent an academic perspective. I trust this information will speak in everyday language and allow you to identify the people in your lives with these traits, so you will know what you are dealing with. I'll offer some suggestions of how to deal with them as well as using tools for self-care as your main focus. In this forewarning, my intention is to empower you to both recognise and manage what can be a painful distraction from your soul's purpose.

Narcissism is not a disorder as was once considered, in recent years it's often referred to as a trait and is referring to (as far as my research has shown) approximately ten to fifteen percent of the population. Keeping in mind it's very difficult to gauge as the measuring tools we have are not great. Another factor that inhibits the statistics is the nature of these people, they are almost always in denial of this trait, which makes it difficult to identify. My sense is, this number is much larger currently on the planet.

As far as I am aware there are five main types of narcissists, I'm going to give a snippet of information about each one:

A) This group are known as the grandiose or overt narcissists. They are all about "look at me", they post their perfect life online or talk about it, they don't ask about you or about your life, unless they've learnt to by observing others and it benefits them in some way. They just talk about themselves, and the most tell-tale sign is they lack empathy; They may have studied the behaviour and act it out at times when expected to, at a funeral for example but they do not feel any empathy. When you look into their eyes, you can see, it's just an act. This is why they behave the way they do. They hate sharing the spotlight with anyone.

B) Far more problematic is the malignant narcissist who demonstrates all the things the overt narcissist does and will also do things that are really mean. They lie or twist the truth which includes damaging a person's name, getting people onside. Sometimes they cheat and steal, they sometimes end up in jail or have affairs. They isolate anyone they consider to be their competition including family members, siblings, even parents.

C) This next type can be surprising to many as they come across as not that confident, they are known as vulnerable or covert narcissists, which means secretive. They are all of the above, as well as reporting how they are "put upon by the world"; always finding their greatness is missed and they say so with a subtle arrogance. Life does them wrong, they say things like, "I do so many great things for the world", implying "no one notices how good I am", "my children are such a problem, why me". They are looking for empathy even though they don't have it for anyone else. They say things like, "when I leave my job, they have to put 3 people on to do what I did," or "I cry myself to sleep because my life is so hard" and are usually passive aggressive. A huge red flag is they are also hyper sensitive to criticism. In my experience all narcissists exhibit this trait, but this type is triggered in an instant. These covert narcissists are often treated for anxiety and mainly depression yet show no improvement from this approach, because this is not the problem. They can be very intellectual in their confrontations, making them the one who knows what's happening because they are so sure of themselves and clever in their communication.

D) This type is known as the communal narcissist. This is the person who does the dog rescue work or drives the neighbour to the medical appointment and makes sure everyone knows about it. They say things like, "look at all the good things I do". "Look at my good work, it's all about giving back". There is no empathy for these things they are helping with, in truth no empathy for anything. "I am above that" is what they believe. They seek a lot of validation for the things they do.

E) The final type is often known as the nice narcissist- This person does all the right things for everyone, they seem so caring and even empathic. Remember empathy can be modelled without feeling. However, if you look closely, you will see the motivation is to have the limelight and gain control. It all looks very "nice", that is until they are not the centre of attention or lose control. Then we get to see what lies beneath the nice exterior. All of this is said without judgement and with an intention for exposing with clarity, that which can be extremely confusing and damaging.

Two of the most common emotions narcissists demonstrate are shame and rage. Shame which is usually supressed or hidden comes from a feeling of having their self-judged flaws exposed. The rage that can be in your face or passive comes from wanting to regain face. They often do this by putting another person down and presenting themselves as superior to feel in control.

If you suspect you have one of these people in your life, it really is worth researching further or enrolling support as it can seem like quite a lot to manage without clarity and a clear pathway. Narcissists can and often do pick-up demonic and parasitic entities that latch to them and use them to drain other people. For sensitive people it can take several days to get over spending time with people demonstrating this trait. It can even cause illness, if it continues unaddressed. It can become a red flag, adding to what we suspect but are not wanting to see.

Your energy can cause havoc in your life because your power magnifies. The strength of the lightworker's energy creates strength in whatever they do, so the chaos can also be great. Sometimes this is a deliberate agenda to stop us from waking up and doing our light work and soul's mission. Have you ever felt like a person drains your lifeforce? Perhaps you just don't feel yourself after spending time with them. These are some of the more obvious red flags and a sign of needing to hold your light stronger and more consciously and then setting new boundaries.

Essentially people with narcissistic traits refuse to self-reflect and take no responsibility for their behaviour. This is largely due to their lack of empathy. If we don't self-reflect and own our behaviour, there is no awareness of a need for change. They need to have positive attention on themselves and will do everything within their power to gain that.

This narcissism can and usually does include gas lighting, so let's look at that trait too before we move on. There are essentially two types of gaslighting: 1) *Soft gaslighting;* for example, when a parent tells their child, "It's not that bad" and if this message stops here, it's simply due to having a misconception that this statement will somehow develop resilience or because the listener feels uncomfortable with the feeling being expressed. As an adult you might be struggling with something and the soft gas lighter says, "that's easy, I don't know anyone who has struggled with that". The message here is more condescending, "there is something wrong with you" but again is an isolated incident.

Then there's malicious and intentional gaslighting: Even though layers of this trait may be unconscious and the gaslighter may not even be aware of what gaslighting is, it's simply in their nature to manipulate people to their advantage. It causes the receiver to lose confidence in who they are, which is more damaging than it sounds.

I am curious about why people do what they do. When you form a negative behaviour, it's often the result of past trauma or something the unconscious mind has developed as a protection. And there really is *no excuse for harmful behaviour* projected at another, we can all choose to do the work. But being aware of this allows for compassion, that also respects your needs. At the same time a realisation of how important setting boundaries is.

When a person acts aggressively towards criticism, and we see them react with narcissism and gas-lighting we are talking about something very different. These are traits and don't tend to change over a lifetime. *A trait is a personal characteristic that reflect a person's internal values and is an aspect of the personality, that are relatively stable over time.* These traits do influence behaviour but do not fully account for behaviour.

Gaslighting can stand alone or be a part of the narcissist way to gain control. Either way narcissistic abuse is one heck of a mean, nasty teacher. The victory is to implement the lessons and move forward.

It's a form of psychological abuse or manipulation and makes you the receiver, question your sanity and who you thought you were. This trait is largely about a power struggle and gaining control and comes from genetics and/or a sense of self-loathing that is never addressed. Seeing you break, sadly, makes them (the gaslighter) feel powerful and better than you.

The people who demonstrate these traits have behaviours in common, both in what they do and in what they say. Knowing these will help eliminate the shock value and help you identify them. Some of the things they say are: "You are too sensitive". "You make a big deal out of everything". They tell you this to get you to back down because it is a big deal. They pinpoint struggles you are having and generalise that you are the problem. They say, "You can't handle things", "*I am trying to help you*"; these statements benefit them by making them look like the helper and you feel insecure. They say, "Your relationships reflect your problems" or "no wonder you don't have many friends". Using other people to back up their story without getting permission or knowing the details. They project their own disowned feelings by calling you angry or say they are not angry. These things are said to make you doubt yourself. They say, you said something that you didn't say, and deny saying something or say I don't recall saying that; to have you question yourself. If you don't do what they want they usually say; "If you really loved me", or "friends, sister's or mothers" for example, "don't act like this"; Essentially, they are invalidating your feelings and trying to manipulate you. This can create deep wounding over time so getting onto this sooner, is highly recommended.

Now let's talk about how you deal with gaslighters. With unintentional gaslighters, even though they will not want you to, take some space from the situation and remember who you are and if you want to, just walk away. With malicious and intentional gaslighters: they tend to isolate you so as not to have witnesses so rather than being abused and hurt again and again, find the strength to walk away. It's not your job to change them and they don't want to change or think they even need to. Seek help to reclaim your sense of self.

But there are also some helpful things to know about this trait; We can't manage what we don't understand:

1) Remain defiant, remember who you are. This is not something that makes you difficult, its being resilient.

2) Recognise there will never be accountability. Addressing this behaviour is harmful, they will never be able to respond to logic and reason. Knowing this gives you back your power. Remember, it's not personal.

3) Letting go of the wish for things to be different.

4) Develop a healthy detachment. I am sure of one thing from my experiences and that is having strong boundaries is an essential part of managing this. I've decided to allow this trait to offer me growth, where it can be so painful, this shifts the focus. It may mean walking away from loved ones or risking being isolated from family. When we truly respect ourselves, we don't allow this abuse in our lives.

5) Many experts on the subject suggest we disengage completely from such an abusive relationship. Sometimes they move away from us, so it resolves itself. Each of us will find our own way. Your way is the way that feels right for you.

In my own journey of being gaslit, I have learnt so much. I've noticed I still have a need for clarity and certainty when making plans. This is largely due to the fact that when we are experiencing gaslighters, especially as a young child, there is no certainty and so later we can develop a need for it, in order to feel safe. This is the protection behaviour I mentioned earlier. "I love you"; "you are the worst person in the world and without me your life is nothing"; they change completely from one time to another, and this is done to stay in charge. The pleasant side of them is often shown when they want something from you and they show the other side when things are not going their way.

The effect can be so great that often the only option that seems available to the subject of the gaslighter or narcissist is suicide or murder. Even as an adult the experience was completely confusing and felt extremely abusive. Before recognising what was happening, in a rampage of rage that was being directed at me, I remember feeling like I wanted to die. For me these feelings of desperation and hopelessness came from the loss of a sense of self and the level of degradation that I experienced. I also remember feeling sadness for the person behind the barrage, it looks like such a dark place to be. I've learnt what gaslighting and narcissism is from the tough teacher of experience, and this has helped me understand myself at a much deeper level.

Organising the experience, writing it down helps validate it. This is real, it happened, and in this process, even if others don't believe you, you remind yourself of who you really are.

Sensitive people have the courage to feel deeply, and this is one of the bravest things we can ever do. Particularly on this planet as it is currently. I think the number one tool is to know who you are and hold onto that strongly and you will get through this. The second tool is the awareness of the strength you gain from challenging experiences. Life happens for me to bring me to who I am today. The overwhelming intention of a narcissist is to gain control over you, over everything. When you say no more, this changes everything, not only in the relationship but in all areas of your life. This is the result of valuing yourself.

You are someone who has seen the truth, and knows you have the power to choose a different path. Exposure is like turning the light on in a dark room. Suddenly everything makes sense. You see the toxic patterns and the ways you have been settling or compromising yourself. And *once you see that, you can't unsee it.* It gives you the ability to take back control of your own life and to break away from situations or people that don't respect or appreciate you. This shift allows you to step forward with a new sense of freedom and purpose.

This is your awakening and no matter how hard it is to see; it is a gift. You get to move forward without the lies and control. To live your life based on who you are, on what you want and on the values you hold. That truly is the greatest freedom there is. Embrace this truth because it is showing what you need to let go of and who you are ready to become. Rather than being controlled, you have been given the gift of clarity, empowerment and freedom.

These people are very good at pulling us into their drama and having us believe they are the ones who make life interesting or exciting but that's an illusion. Some people come into our lives to help us to grow, like a difficult course of study. Necessary for growth development and learning but not the main narrative. Narcissist come into our life to teach us certain truths and to test our ability to hold onto our power. They show us what happens when we ignore our boundaries. When we prioritize someone else's needs and opinions above our own and let go of our worth just to keep the peace. They show us what we don't want so we can move forward with clarity towards what we do want.

When you understand these things, you start to see their role differently and you stop feeling like you need to fix them or save them or make them change. Instead, you realise, they've played their part. *They've exposed patterns, insecurities, and unresolved issues within you that needed healing.* **They've done their job.**

Now it's your turn to write the next chapter, with a new focus on yourself. On your growth and on your peace. Once you see they were never meant to be the central focus, you can let go. You can release them without guilt, without regret and without the need for closure because that comes from understanding their role and knowing that they've served it.

This can be a good time to remind yourself of the power of your focus. Joining the dots to see your relationships in their true light gives you the opportunity to look after yourself moving forward. Firstly, while remembering the power of what you are attracting through where your beliefs and thoughts are focused, and secondly, we are never responsible for other people's bad or unhealthy behaviour. But when we are ready the universe often uses our experiences to teach us what we are ready to learn, regardless of our focus.

What keeps us on track even though there are many hurdles on our path as lightworkers or sacred beings, is our commitment to our souls' mission. What's been happening every time you've been tempted or seen a morally questionable path to take, you've chosen not to.

You've said, I'll take the humble road where I can live with myself and you've done this time and time again, all through your life. It doesn't mean you haven't slipped up, you haven't been perfect. I haven't been perfect yet we've been incorruptible at a soul level. Regardless of what you've been through that's what has kept you on your soul's path.

Some highly sensitive humans are also Seers. This is often included in the energy of a Blue Ray, Indigo and Empath. It is less common than some sensitive types, it seems to me around one in every hundred thousand. Seers intuitively see and know things that most people don't. In the realm of spirituality, a Seer holds a unique and revered position.

They're often described as an observer; a Seer is someone who possesses a heightened sensitivity to the unseen forces at play in the universe, and is attuned to subtle energies and spiritual dimensions that shape our reality. A Seer approaches their role with humility and openness, they understand the future is not set in stone but rather a tapestry of possibilities waiting to unfold.

As an observer, a Seer watches these possibilities with keen interest, offering insights and guidance based on their deep connection to the spiritual realms. Throughout history, Seers have played vital role in guiding individuals and community on their spiritual journeys. They serve as conduits between the physical and the spiritual worlds offering wisdom and clarity in times of need. For a Seer, sometimes the future becomes clear before it happens. Sometimes the universe gives us hints about things before they happen. This can be like a warning signal telling us to pay attention. If you find yourself sensing something bad might occur and feel you need to do something about it, or you see an event before it happens, you might be a Seer. It's like you have a sixth sense. The universe communicates in mysterious ways. Sometimes dropping little clues or signs for us to pick up on. As a Seer you might notice these signs more than other people do.

It's like having an inner radar that alerts you to potential dangers or troubles ahead. This ability to be able to see the future may start off as a glimpse and expand, like the gifts developed over many lifetimes often do. This future seeing is both a gift and a responsibility. Imagine you're walking down the street and you suddenly choose to stop walking. It's the universe kicking in and making you stop, letting you know there is danger ahead. You avoid this danger because you listen to the message. The signs are often subtle but their purpose it to protect you and others. It feels like you are being guided by a higher power, that nudges you from deep in your soul and shows you the right direction.

Synchronicities are meaningful coincidences that happen in our lives and for Seers they can be particularly significant. They're not just about noticing patterns and connections, but it's about recognising the hand of the universe at work. These synchronicities might appear as repeating numbers on a clock or in your environment, e.g., 10.10, 11.11, 4.44 or chance encounters with people or unexpected opportunities seem to align perfectly with your desires. It's like breadcrumbs are being left by the universe urging us to pay attention and follow the signs.

As a child, even without having the words, I remember feeling connected to God, (the name I used back then) the angels and to spirituality. If you have these connections, it is another sign that you might be a Seer. It's like having a

LORINA

natural inclination to understand things beyond what you can see.

From your early years in life, you might have been drawn to concepts like love, kindness, or the idea of something much bigger than us. For example: I always enjoyed doing the forty-hour famine as a child and asked everyone I knew to sponsor me, to help the children who didn't have enough food in Africa. It just made no sense to me that children would be starving. I remember as a child sitting with Jack, a friend of my Mum and Dad's for hours just listening to him talk because he was lonely, and the rest of the family would vanish because they found it difficult. I also remember sponsoring a child in a third world country and becoming a member of Green-Peace as soon as I had an income. These were things I was drawn to early in life. We naturally care for everything and everyone.

This connection to caring, to spirituality isn't something everyone feels strongly, but for the Lightworker it feels like your foundation, and it's always been a part of your life. You may also have found solace in nature, felt connected to animals, or had moments of profound insight.

Another sign of being a Seer is a persistent feeling of not quite fitting in or belonging to the world around you. You sense you're from somewhere else or that your true home lies beyond the confines of this earthly realm.

This feeling of displacement is compounded for Seers as they often sense limitations of the physical world and yearn for a deeper connection to the spiritual dimensions. This feeling of not belonging includes feeling out of sync with societal norms and expectations, struggling to find like-minded individuals who understand their spiritual journey, or experiencing a higher state of consciousness beyond the mundane realities of life. Just as difficult experiences are designed to do, this struggle serves as a powerful catalyst to spiritual growth and self-discovery.

It feels like being a seed who has been planted in unfamiliar soil, striving to find nourishment and connection amidst the uncertainty of your surroundings. You might find solace in knowing that your true home lies within the depths of your soul, where you are eternally connected to the infinite wisdom and love of the universe.

Being a Seer is not about having super natural powers or having all the answers, it offers us clues to our deeper purpose and deeper connection to the world around us. Who you are will unfold in your life a bit at a time, to allow you time to reconnect with and integrate these parts.

It's like piecing together a puzzle, each sign revealing a new piece of the picture until you begin to see the larger whole. Whether you connect all of your qualities or just some, staying open to the spiritual realms will allow you to feel connected and supported.

You may have a few of these Seer signs or perhaps many of them. There are many over lapping traits to the HSP's but they are a larger section of the population. This way of being is not a conscious choice, it feels more like who we are and all that we have been through has moulded us into this.

It can be a blessing and a curse being a HSP, until we learn to understand, embrace and more importantly learn to accept it as a part of ourselves. Many sensitive people are living with personal rejection or denial of their sensitivity, and this is largely due to the fact that it is often judged as a fault and goes unacknowledged in our society as a strength. The main block and most damaging that I experienced personally, until I began to wake up in my late twenties, early thirties, was rejecting that part of myself. We are this uniqueness. We can run, we can hide but it will not go away because unless we embrace who we are, we can never truly know ourselves, live a functional life, or complete our mission. All of it is a part of our divine magic. All of it is required to fulfill our divine mission.

Many HSP feel it's a burden, as feeling everything so deeply demands that we embrace it. For us to have a happy, healthy, functioning life, who we are, demands we own all of it. Many of us dabble in shutting our feelings down to avoid the personal work required to live authentically. Through the pain this road leads most of us to choose, eventually, to bring it out of the shadow and into the light and fully own this aspect of ourselves. Recognising our gifts that come with this heightened sensitivity, helps us make sense of our world and feel empowered. Many of us can read people's belongings, especially jewellery known as Psychometry, even if we've just met them. Our radar for lies or other people's B.S. is absolute. We can pick dodgy or dishonest behaviour and energy in an instant and can feel people's energy, even if we are not in their company.

We feel very deeply so it can be tempting to shut down, as I did as a child and teenager. With the amount of unacknowledged dysfunction in families and relationships, and as a result all the unhealed wounding that is being projected in many environments, our world is not an easy place to be. Especially when we feel everything, so deeply. This wounding creates a harsh environment that HSP's find very challenging to manage. Until we HSP own and embrace this aspect of ourselves, it can feel a bit like a choice to sink or swim.

My own experience of suppression and judging this part of myself was because in my younger years I didn't have the skills to manage it. I felt that I was too sensitive and hard work for myself and others. This denial led me to having anxiety and panic attacks as my body's wisdom did all it could to get my attention. Supressing our feelings causes many problems, and they are designed to let us know we are missing the wisdom of our own guidance system and that we are off track for our life.

I saw this time as an opportunity to choose whether I broke down or broke through. I was either going to own and embrace my uniqueness of being an HSP or end up dependent on the broken health system, while living a dysfunctional or disempowered life. Gratefully, I found the courage to allow my life's path to lead me to making the choice to own all parts of myself. All of them, including my feelings, which are communication from my soul. They are an essential part of us, especially for us HSP's. This is something that deeply supports our life. I was like a feather in the wind without it.

Owning ourselves and accepting both the shadow and the light exactly as we are, is the key to healthy self-worth, wholeness, peace and evolution. It's also the path to a functioning, healthy and fulfilling life, not only for HSP's but for everyone. I am grateful and feel blessed to say, I know myself better today than I ever have. With the blessing of life being a mirror of ourselves, my practice as a Clinical Hypnotherapist attracts many highly sensitive people who I feel completely privileged to work with. I find these people, kind, caring, compassionate, gentle, as well as courageous and strong. They are almost always in some type of a caretaking role and that can look quite different from the outside, a bicycle repairer, a child care worker, a hairdresser, a parent, a friend, a daughter, a son, an accountant, a teacher or a therapist. Being a human being offers this role of caring for each other to us all to use however we choose to or are able.

The reason I mentioned HSP's strength is that many people see being sensitive as a weakness, when the truth is it takes great courage to be sensitive in this world. It is a strength that runs very deep, to have the courage to feel the pain and suffering of this planet. We also struggle because we are living in a world that has all but lost its capacity and value in feeling and connection with each other. This struggle can often show up in feelings of isolation and loneliness, as many of us retreat from a world that seems quite foreign and even confusing a lot of the time.

In the evolution of my experience as being an HSP, one of the greatest learnings I've taken away is that if something I feel from another person sticks to me then I still have some work to do in that area, as there must be some of it within me. Otherwise, it is felt for a short time and then I alchemise it. If I feel like my energy is being drained, again this is feedback and something I am responsible for letting happen. When I am connected to my body, I notice this, and can support myself or remove myself.

Resistance is the unconscious mind's role of protection, and we can have resistance to anything. A trigger is an overwhelmingly strong emotion that comes up when we have experienced something similar to a past trauma that hasn't been acknowledged or healed. The unconscious mind mistakenly thinks it still needs to protect you from it now, this is because it has no concept of time. Resistance shows up as negative emotions, a fear of one type or another- jealousy, stubbornness, projection, anxiety etc or even over thinking because all fears are resistance, and *all negative emotion comes through the mind.* Remember the story of the Japanese soldiers?

These behaviours and tell-tale signs often show up in HSP when they disown these sensitive parts of themselves. As we become aware of the value of knowing and accepting ourselves, this ownership allows us to become more of who we are.

Any personal issues or triggers require us to firstly feel them, by owning the experience and, secondly releasing them by consciously letting go. *To feel, is to heal.*

Recognising the energy as belonging to another is not always easy. What is mine and what is theirs? That's why self-awareness is so vital. Merging with another's energy can be useful information especially if we are working as a healer or therapist as it gives us insights as to what is happening with our client. Although this can only be of assistance if they are willing to do the work and own these feelings. The work is simpler than we might believe. Be in the moment, feel your feelings, and without buying into the story in your head or any resistance, be willing to let go.

Even though many HSP's find their lives challenging, our world needs them, just as we need our frogs. They/we hold the people of our world accountable and offer an ancient perception and understanding of both oneness and connection. We are the healers; the carriers of light and unity consciousness and we demonstrate by our very existence that humanity is a group species.

All of our thoughts, actions and energy affect the whole of humanity, known also as the collective, and this occurs within every moment of our lives, whether we are conscious of it or not. Intention is the primary energy that the universe responds to. We can be gentle and kind or strong and assertive but when the underlying intention is love, towards ourselves and others, then the vibration of love is what we create.

For those who feel deeply, compassion is your gift but it's also your learning tool. When you have the gift of truly seeing people, you can find beauty in anyone. In relationship this may lead you to justify hurtful behaviour because you see the heart behind it and the pain it's coming from. Seeing their humanity is an incredible quality but as my life has taught me, it doesn't excuse their behaviour. You can be lovingly and fiercely compassionate and wise.

Enabling is not kindness, not for you or the other person. You can step into your own warrior that demands truth, honour and respect. Remember you are the primary protector of your own heart. Hold yourself with the deep self-respect and love you deserve. That might look like creating distance as your answer to disrespect. Rather than reacting, arguing, diving into drama, you might simply remove your presence.

Sensitive people have an infinite connection to nature and are usually drawn to water. Within everybody of water is a spirit that most often cannot be seen. It's as if they sense the spirit and benefit from the peace it offers. Perhaps that is why so many of us prefer to live or holiday either on or near the water. We humans are mostly water, around 73%, the same percentage as our planet, which can serve to remind us of our connection to her. I find it fascinating that the water we drink could be the same water that Mahalia Jackson or Jesus drank, it just keeps being recycled. It is a large part of our makeup, and it can reflect much about a human when we look deeply into it. Water is intelligent, it's a feeling source of energy and one which is vital to life on this planet. Water is an element that holds history, memories, emotions and the subtle mysteries of the psyche. It raises in vibration as the planet does. When you allow yourself to go with the flow of life, and become as honest and as clear as water, you will see your life flourish.

Throughout the universes, there are many dimensions of experience, which our scientific data struggles to keep up with. My sense is we haven't been ready until now. Mainly because, if our universes are different from what we have been told then, where does that leave the concept of ourselves within these universes. Within these experiences of creation there are many dimensions from the third to the thirty-sixth, each one bringing new levels of awareness and experience. In the spiritual circles of information, we hear mostly about the dimensions three to twelve. Planet earth, that is relatively new in the scheme of the Universe, has been experiencing 3D reality for many thousands of years, since the sinking of Lemuria and Atlantis. Since then, the energy or vibration of this planet has been dense and fear based.

Earth and her inhabitants have been functioning on a perception that we are separate from each other as well as the Source of Creation or the Divine. This perception has led us to the pain we inflict on ourselves and each other. This planet has been a great school for learning, particularly learning about our individuality. Our destiny was always to create a planet where all live in harmony, unity and love.

The non-benevolent intruders of the past resulting in this collective conditioning has kept the human being under control by disempowering us and hiding information, including that of our full potential. Most of the world sleeps while this continues however, there is an ever-increasing number of us waking up to the truth.

When we open our eyes, we can see how this illusionary belief of separateness has led us all to isolation, loneliness, fears, wars, illness, taking our own life, pain, poverty and destruction of each other, ourselves and of the planet herself. The good news is there is a great shift taking place and sensitive people are some of those who are on the front line. I will continue to discuss this shift in greater detail in the chapters to come, and each chapter is intended to be a step of awareness in this direction. All of creation is changing and evolving and here on earth this change is being referred to as a dimensional shift from the 3D, through 4D and into the 5D.

The shift is about learning to love yourself first and then expanding this love vibration out to everything and everyone. This self-love is a journey of self-discovery where we uncover our shadow-self, the aspects of our personality that are often judged as wrong and shameful and embrace them as a part of us. Loving our best self is quite easy but in order to love everyone, we must learn to love every part of ourselves. This is another example of a microcosm of the macrocosm and oneness. Love is inclusive, and loving all parts of us is naturally followed by loving all of creation.

Externally there are challenges to come, much of our world is in turmoil and change can be a rough ride but the good news is this process is destined to occur within our lifetime. There is nothing to fear as everything is happening through us and for us and our greater good.

Formattable change will appear on the horizon as though it would unseat humanity, triggering fears, with many more firsts and unchartered waters, without present clarification of events. Things will not appear this way for those awakened, this will be experienced differently by you. When you are awakened, the internal vibration that you house becomes louder, it speaks to you with new force and takes on new meaning. You may call this connection spirit, higher-self, your guides or the Divine. You have a knowing that no matter how things look, all is in order.

You will not succumb to the experience of the suffering and degradation as you have surrendered fear and are fear free. It cannot stick to you any longer. The sensitives amongst us may still feel the pain that we see before us but we have learnt to find a place for it, by trusting in the divine plan. Life will be experienced with a

INCONVENIENT CONSCIOUSNESS

great dynamic of interdependence of relying on each other being born anew. Remember this: a powerful new experience of being human is birthing and unity consciousness will prevail.

We humans are an extraordinary species, with a body and mind that can, with the right focus and understanding, heal itself. We have an intellect that has access to universal intelligence. Darwin's theory has never been supported by fossil evidence that we evolved from Apes. I do however, support evolution as a concept and we can see this throughout nature. Since around 200-300,00 years ago when humans showed up, there has been questions about our origins. We are beings who have unlimited potential, more than we were ever aware of, with the recognition of the twenty-fourth pair of chromosomes. We were told a long time ago that our DNA controlled everything and we are limited by it. Thank fully with the help of biological science our knowledge has come a long way. Now we understand more about the function of what used to be called junk DNA. Science had no idea what function these huge pieces if DNA had. We now know these strands of DNA are switched on and off through our thoughts and emotions.

Many indigenous cultures or those I have researched have a common teaching. This includes the traditional people of central China and Tibet, the monks, nuns and mystics in Nepal and India, the monks of Thailand, the first people's traditions in the Andes mountains in Peru, the San tribes of Africa and the Australian First Nations People. Everyone of those groups teach their young, "we are related to an intelligence beyond this physical planet". Hearing this may not have any impact on you and of course you are free to decide what you believe and what feels right for you. Either way this opens up a broader view of our potential.

IORINA

When we are in our original vibration of love, we have an intuitive ability to know innately how to govern ourselves. We know that we can live a life of joy, abundance, unity and well-being without being dictated to. However, we have been lied to since we took our first breath, so in order to reclaim our birth right of who we really are, each of us has to be prepared to do the work to make the journey of waking up to the truth of who we are. It can be done any way we prefer, that's our free-will in action but if feels like the timing of it for each individual is not a conscious choice. Rather, it feels more predestined, something each of us planned before incarnating, that fits into the bigger picture. The world requires stability to some degree and if everyone was waking up together and facing our fears, there would be turmoil and bedlam everywhere. Even more than is currently happening.

This bedlam can play out in large worldwide events or in our personal life. Just over a year ago, I had an experience where a neighbour and I were discussing a change that was coming up in their life. After they told me about their options for this change, I replied with what I felt could be a potential hurdle and the choice that I would make if it were mine to make. This was not received as I intended it. Although we had shared a friendship for many years, at this time and as this event unfolded it became evident, we were triggering each other's wounding. When the soul is ready, the vibrational agreement shows up.

There are periods in our life usually somewhere in our early 30's, 60's and 90's, when we experience what is known as a Saturn return. This is when Saturn returns to the degree in its orbit that it was at your time of birth. This planet's purpose is to stir things up, a person crosses over a major threshold and enters the next stage of life. It

INCONVENIENT CONSCIOUSNESS

brings what has remained hidden from our unconscious into our conscious awareness, to help us wake up to what is limiting us or keeping us stuck from our full potential. Its purpose is to help us move forward. We both fitted into these age groups.

As I continued to talk with this person, I noticed there seemed to be a resistance to receiving guidance. I had felt something was off but was unable to pinpoint its true nature. It can be an interesting time when what was once hidden becomes obvious. It is largely due to our shifts in consciousness but also as it is the age of Aquarius. A time of change, exposure, hope and innovation. My life has taught me to bring any negative emotions that I experience back to myself, that way we can be around unhealthy behaviour and remain grounded and calm. Saying this co-exists with not being responsible for other people's degrading or abusive behaviour. In this instant I became aware of a negative response inside of me, a trigger, and I had a strong need to have them understand my intentions. On reflection, I can see how both of our perceptions and our unconscious wounding's were making the same event seem different and uncomfortable for each of us. Therefore, it presented a possibility for growth, for both of us. We react rather than respond from wounding that usually occurs in childhood or earlier lives, when these wounds are left unhealed. There's always a choice to project the negative emotions, resulting from the wounding, out to the person we are interacting with, or to own them.

The first clue in self-reflection for my wound was the urge to have my intentions understood. I had feelings of sadness and fear come up, so I knew I had some work to do. Negative emotions are always resistance. This fear was so strong that it stopped me from speaking up, I just went quiet. I knew there was something for me to explore here, when I was able.

Triggers, although challenging in nature, are a blessing when we are living a conscious life and are self-aware because they lead us to healing. But they are almost always very painful because they present themselves with big emotions to gain our attention. I'm sure I could have explained myself more clearly to this person without fear, if I was conscious of what this was triggering for me, but this is rarely the case with triggers. That being said, I still respect a person's request and unless someone asks for help, it's not my place to give it. I misunderstood the talk to mean they were wanting a second opinion. I knew this logically but regardless of knowing this, I had an unreasonable urge to explain my motivation. I felt misunderstood and that really bothered me. It became obvious to me that we were both being triggered.

It seems to me that everything is either an anchor or a trigger. An anchor is an existing behaviour or emotion that you can attach to a new behaviour or habit you are building. For example, when I am about to do public speaking, I remember the time I felt confident and performed my best: "The day I went sky diving was one of the best days I can remember, I was confident and empowered". The habit of brushing your teeth is anchored to waking up in the morning: "Every morning after I wake up, I brush my teeth".

If you have ever experienced a trigger, I'm sure this will resonate. If you haven't, it is something you simply cannot ignore. A trigger is an emotional reminder we get from having a similar experience that caused us to form a limited/fear-based belief that we store in our unconscious mind. It's a belief that we decide is true. We created it by what we made the event mean. It happened at a traumatic time in our life, and through our own filter of perception we built a limited belief to match our meaning. Our unconscious mind doesn't refer to time, so everything is happening now, the past trauma and this one.

The unconscious mind makes the world match up with our beliefs, its purpose is to help us make sense of the world and to protect us. For example, if you experienced criticism as a child, you can make people wanting to help you mean a number of things, depending on your wound; "People think I can't think for myself", or "I am stupid", or "I am unlovable", or that "There's something wrong with me", or "No-one understands me", or "I am not enough" or perhaps the limited belief is something completely different. It all depends on the persons meaning or perception at the time of wounding.

Nothing means anything. Let me explain. If there is a day where it rains, and I am an event's organiser: "Wet days are so inconvenient. The rain spoils everything. I'll have to move to a new venue. I hate wet weather." or if I'm a gardener I can make it mean: "When it rains, I'm so happy because it waters my garden, and I love the sound of rain on the roof. I love rain".

It's just a day with rain, it's the meaning we give it that changes everything. When a child makes a situation mean, "I am being criticised", "I'm letting my parent down" if they express being unhappy with me and a similar situation arises, it triggers this wounding. Although we can blame the person who reminds us of the wound, saying, "You triggered me". They are just the messenger. It's being brought up to be felt with the purpose of healing it. They didn't put it inside of you, you did and only you can release it. I see it as a blessing because every trigger identified and healed gives us more freedom to be who we really are, without those self-imposed limitations.

Nothing means anything until we give it meaning and this meaning is most often created by us as a child. It is developed from the thinking of a child and makes perfect sense to that child. It's the meaning we give it that forms the belief. Until we own this fear-based belief and not everyone is ready or willing to do that, we usually project it out at others through blame, e.g., you as the criticised child becomes critical of others. A good example of this is shown in the poem, "Children learn what they live" which can be found online. This poem highlights some of the wounding's almost all of us have experienced in childhood and the result of those wounds.

When a fear-based belief exists in our unconscious mind and is running us just like a computer program runs the computer, it can and usually does feel like it's out of our control. The events and people in our life have to match up with our belief so that our world makes sense. For example, the world will confirm to me what I believe, even if that was not the intention of the world. Helping becomes criticising.

In order to match experiences with our unconscious beliefs, we usually need to unconsciously distort, delete, and generalise events to match whatever we believe. Have you ever thought someone said something, that they completely deny saying and they were not in resistance. I know I have. That's a good example of distorting information to suit what we believe about the world. When a fear is unconscious or active in our unconscious mind, it controls our behaviour. It has yet to be owned and is therefore a shadow trait and not in our conscious awareness, so we continue to be at the effect of it and suffer until it becomes conscious. The suffering it causes is designed to get our attention. Our desire to become conscious often manifests into struggles so we move in the direction of our greatest good. This is one of the values of struggle. It often forces us to face what we have been avoiding and then experience the growth that comes from that.

INCONVENIENT CONSCIOUSNESS

When we live unconsciously, we act unconsciously too. An example of unconscious behaviour is: We can "forget" to do something that is important to the person who was triggering us because in our unconscious, we blame them and therefore they are the cause of our pain. We can crash a car, burn a meal, miss an appointment, miss their birthday, post photos on social media excluding them or even go no contact, excluding them from our life unless we need them. All or any of these events can be a form of unconscious payback. Especially if you are unconscious of your triggers or what they are or are unwilling to own them. This can result in you wanting to blame and to feel resentment.

The experience I mentioned before triggered me, I felt misunderstood and that felt very scary for me. This negative reaction meant my unconscious mind has a fear-based belief that connects me to being misunderstood with something that felt so scary, it actually felt life threatening. The meaning I gave this situation was that "I am unsafe if people misunderstand me". Now I know logically that I am safe with my family member even if they do not understand me, but the unconscious mind is not logical. It has no concept of time and only knows this thing that is happening is like that other thing that caused angst and stress. At that time, I had been experiencing several incidents where I was misunderstood, and I was unreasonably unsettled by this.

That's the blessing of living consciously- we self-reflect and when things are not loving and harmonious, we know these are a wounding showing up to be healed. There is usually a limited belief from our inner child at play when we are in conflict, and the key is how it affects us. More specifically, how we feel. If we feel negative emotions or get drawn in, it is a personal wounding.

When we move towards an upgrade in our awareness, our life often shows us anything that has been holding us back. The question I had for myself was how can I be my best self, while carrying this fear? For me, the fear of being misunderstood sat beneath my fear of not speaking up, playing small, not allowing myself to be successful or even noticed. That explained my life up until this moment. Even though I am a very capable person, I have demonstrated self-sabotage, hiding, running away, anything I could do to fit my life into this belief and to feel safe. The thing is, we can never really feel safe when we are allowing fear to control us. Although all of this felt a little challenging and overwhelming, I knew I had the courage to face myself and I wanted to be free. With all of my heart I want this relationship to be conscious, harmonious and loving but I can only do my part. Unconditionally loving another can co-exist with boundaries about tolerance for unhealthy behaviour.

I know logically that I'm not responsible for other people's understandings or perceptions of me and that I'm safe even if they misunderstand me, but as previously mentioned, the *unconscious mind is not logical*. I was nothing short of petrified by the thought of it.

Self-care is an essential part of living consciously, just as it is caring for others. I can't be there for another if I'm not here for myself.

The anxious feeling I had was a trigger. This was a negative memory stored in my unconscious mind that was calling out to me to acknowledge it, release and replace it with what I want for my life.

As time unfolded, I uncovered a fear of being misunderstood and this one was from a past life. It was a pattern that has limited my life for as long as I can remember. Due to my experience of accessing limited beliefs, I was able to clarify what my pattern was fuelled by. I anchored a belief in my unconscious mind from past experiences; "If people misunderstand me, I will die in a very painful way".

It was a belief left over from past lives, and many have become a conscious memory for me. Lives of persecution and being tortured and killed for being a light worker, a Sharman or just someone with *unusual powers*. Many light workers have limited beliefs and patterns of behaviour that is the result of these past traumas. We were often the scapegoat for events that couldn't be explained. Things like famines, floods, the spread of an illness, misfortune that befell the royals for example, as well as not partaking in community expectation that was non benevolent. I have an ability to remember and often see past lives and I'm grateful for that, it helps in the releasing process.

Many spiritual warriors have this fear of being persecuted because of our past experiences, that is, until we acknowledge it which diminishes its power and we're then able to let it go. Essentially, we do this by realising, and reminding ourselves *that was then, and this is now* and things are different in a good way. I was fortunate to be able to do this with the help of a colleague. This is a great reminder of the craziness of judging another person when they exhibit behaviour that we don't understand. I'm not talking about setting boundaries for your wellbeing, I'm talking about judging people, this is very different. Judging is about making someone or their behaviour wrong because you know what is right. Not only do we delete and distort things to suit what we believe, we just don't have all the information to judge anyone.

I'd like to share with you how my colleague and I were able to release this belief. And just as there are many types of people in the world, there are many ways to

resolve things that hold us back in our lives. This is one:
I explained the situation to my colleague. We began by focusing on the area of my body that I felt the fear of being misunderstood. It was in my solar plexus chakra, just below my heart. As I did that, I noticed a feeling of resistance to letting it go. Remember the unconscious mind is only ever trying to look after and protect us and it needs to know you will be ok without this protection. I then focused on letting the resistance go, layer upon layer. I said, "This resistance is really gripping on and it feels like a huge battle". As I talked to this resistant part of me, I could feel it served a purpose. It thought staying there was vital to my survival.

In that moment, it came to me to say, "You are causing me more trouble hanging on to this fear than I would experience being without it". In that moment, almost like a wave of magic washed over me, everything changed. The resistance and the fear felt like a wave departing. They just dissolved. There was a blanket of peace that gently washed over me, and I knew I was free.

I was amazed and delighted how this part of me cared so deeply about protecting me. As it released the resistance by hearing my reassurance that I am safe to make this change, it allowed my balance to return. As I released the fear, my life regained harmony and my heart opened wider.

It's worth mentioning that most therapists, regardless of their discipline, cannot successfully work on themselves. We all need a little help from someone else and I love that. I've asked many practitioners: chiropractors, psychologists, counsellors, kinesiologists, hypnotherapist and others, it seems to apply to almost everyone. It feels like the universe is reminding us that we too can ask and get the help we need. We are all moving towards being free of *all fears* to become *all love again,* where nothing, can ever, trigger us again.

INCONVENIENT CONSCIOUSNESS

Leonardo DaVinci spoke about the different perceptions of humans when he said, "There is an esoteric truth about the three natures of humans: 1) Those who see, 2) Those who see when shown and 3) Those who don't see.

Everyone is on a different journey, often on different time lines and sharing different vibrations and as a result this is not a global awakening, rather, an individual choice. "Those who see" or are awake can assist group two, "those who see when shown" and this group of people are the planets greatest potential for change. We cannot control the lessons, development and free will of anyone and we can only assist those who ask us. The way to identify "those who don't see" and are just happily or unhappily living an unconscious life, is to be authentically yourself. Feel how you are when you spend time with them and to see where things lead. Are they moving towards understanding, love and unity or control, fear and separation.

Sometimes you might be taken by surprise and have to adjust your intention from one of honesty or supporting, to one of accepting and allowing things to be just as they are. This may require you to step back or set boundaries. There may even be a healing in it for you, as this example above showed me.

Not everyone chooses higher consciousness. Once you know which group of people you are dealing with, you can take one of these three approaches while demonstrating your acceptance of every soul having the right to be where they are:

1) "Those who don't see": These are often newer souls that have yet to understand; that what we give out comes back to us. Boundaries for us around projections and unconscious behaviours are often required. Largely supporting this group is around acceptance, setting boundaries and holding our light strongly so that we can

be and give love even if that looks like tough love. All of this is done while respecting our own and others' long-term wellbeing.

2) "Those who see when shown": Even though this group is usually open to growth and self-reflection it's still important to wait to be asked for support. When these people ask, they are ready and willing to do the work and it's a pleasure to work with them.

3) "Those who see": are still on a journey but are most often open to self-reflection and growth and come from a place of service. They often love to share deep conversation with others who also see.

When we set boundaries with any of these people, they are not to escape triggers but are intended to lovingly allow things to unfold in the most compassionate way for everyone involved. When a fear-based belief has formed in a person's unconscious mind, but they are unaware of it or unwilling to do their work of ownership, then their projections can be unhelpful, even detrimental for everyone concerned. This leaves us with choices while we continue to hold this person in our heart with love.

If the person who sees is unable to set boundaries and practice self-care, then this is often a sign of self-blame or non-forgiveness, and there is something more to become conscious of and some inner work to do.

I struggled to set boundaries in this earlier situation, and it became evident that I had some self-forgiveness work to do. I had additional limited beliefs to what I was consciously aware of, where I was judging myself. Self-judgement causes feelings of shame and guilt and can keep us accepting less than we deserve. This process was necessary so that I could lovingly step back from this person for now and accept where they are at, while showing myself and them respect and love. Following your heart doesn't always look pretty and it isn't always what everyone thinks is ok. It is however always for the highest good of all. It is action motivated by love.

We make shifts by letting go of old outdated beliefs and stories of how we are somehow unworthy of the best in life, and this is done by recognising those limitations. We can only heal something that we acknowledge is present in our life.

As you identify any area of your life that is not working, you'll be sure to find a limited belief in your unconscious mind that is running you. As I explored my wounding, I discovered this limited belief came from some of my earliest memories. I recalled many incidences of being told by my father without any ill intention, "Your mother bottle fed you and you were a bad baby because you didn't keep the milk down". He told me how I would projectile vomit five bottles before keeping one down. As we understand now, I had a dairy intolerance.

That must have been so difficult for everyone, including Mum and myself. I can only imagine how tired my Mum must have been. Dad said, "she would cry with tiredness" and he again reminded me, how "bad" I was.

Back in those days in the 1960's little was known about unusual conditions of children's health, their mind development, emotional needs, and imprinting, sensitivities, allergies or even feeding options for babies. I would have picked up messages from both parents as a baby, even before I could speak a language, that they were not happy with me. A baby knows when they are loved and when they are a bother by the feelings exchanged, by eye contact or lack thereof, by the type of physical contact or lack of it and for a HSP, by the feelings.

The developmental stage of our brain in our early years is such that we believe everything happens because of us. We are the centre of our world. As I became more conscious, I acknowledged and gratefully understood where these patterns of behaviour originated. My parents were doing their best, with the knowledge they had at the time, as all people do ... but the seed was sewn. This is a great example of how beliefs are formed; Even before my father said the words, "You were a bad baby, you caused your mother so many problems", I felt it from my mum. I have carried a deep feeling of not having my needs met, that they don't matter. I grew up believing "I was bad" and "I was a nuisance" and that makes perfect sense with the messages I would have received. I have struggled to ask for help or stand up for myself partly due to these beliefs. I did everything I could to make my world fit these meanings I had given my life, as we all do. That's why changing limiting beliefs and patterns are life changing. I'm sharing this not to parent bash, it is the most challenging of roles. My intention is to highlight how we develop these limited beliefs.

I had no idea I even had these beliefs until well into my conscious journey that I began in my early 30's. These beliefs fuelled my life unconsciously, as they do for all of us. In order for me to know these beliefs or any others were in my mind, I had to play them out, become aware of their existence and then own them.

On reflection when I spent time away from my children, when they lived with their dad, this fitted my beliefs at the time. Even though this time and these events served many purposes for everyone involved. At the time my conscious intentions, those I was aware of, were to help humanity, I can now see some unconscious beliefs were being made true; It became obvious how it was also fuelled by this belief: Only a "bad" mother who was a nuisance would do such a thing.

All of this has served me, and everyone involved. Every experience has a gem of wisdom to offer us, a learning. The learning is usually opposite to the limited belief we choose from our conditioning of being separate. For example, the learning I uncovered in order to heal from the belief "I am bad" is: "I am worthy, I am loved unconditionally, I am love". There is no right or wrong learning just the one that feels right for you. All experiences serve us, that's why compassion for our journey, no matter how it has looked, is how we set ourselves free. Compassion is love with understanding. Free from judgement and free from guilt. My independence is largely fuelled by the belief in being a nuisance. That can be seen as a positive result when I balance it with being able to allows others in, during times of need. That has been a challenge for me. I'm still learning to ask for help as some beliefs take their own time to shift.

We cannot change limited patterns or beliefs by only using affirmations, we must allow time for new pathways to develop in our minds. The new belief I chose is I am supported by the universe. The exciting shift is, that this new belief is now showing up in my life, more and more often.

When you bring to your awareness anything that causes you to struggle, you can identify a faulty thought process fuelled by a limited belief and pattern of behaviour. In identifying this, you can then surrender the egos need to control and be right. And all the stories and justifications you tell yourself to make the belief correct while staying righteously stuck.

This process of letting go is done through being present, here and now in our life as it is. Humility helps us to let go of being right, which is a false power of the ego, and face the parts of ourselves we have been afraid of or have judged. *We have freewill, a choice to be right or to be happy, which are you choosing?* Ask yourself, how much better can this get? It's a great question for all of life's experiences. The universe responds to our intentions and will respond to this question by showing you better and better versions.

We can bring any discordant emotions from the past to our conscious awareness and fully own them by feeling them. Not for hours or days like the past but to fully feel our feelings allows them to move through in just 90 seconds. The hard slog is over, the path is cut. We will visit the Karmic and Dharmic paths until we make the shift. The Dharmic path is when we are able to learn from life in the present, as it unfolds. It is one of the blessings of doing the work.

Nothing is personal unless we have a wound that is triggered by an experience, understanding where people are coming from allows us to relate to them in a more suitable way for all involved. As we let go of fear and learn to love ourselves more unconditionally, we choose relationships that are kind, regardless of the consciousness level of the people involved, we also love others unconditionally. Sometimes that looks like loving them from a distance, but the love is constant. Saying that, consciousness is love and is a part of the person so becomes a part of any relationship the conscious person enters. The key here is consciousness. It is the essential ingredient for genuine empathy and kindness.

A relationship of two people creates three energies. Each person creates an energy and there is a third energy that is created by the coming together of these two individuals. We can even help heal a relationship that is struggling by using a process of filling the three energies with light but, essentially, it's the free-will of each person that determines where the relationship goes in a physical sense. Some relationships come to a completion as one or both people release old karmic agreements. Most often this happens for one person and the other can find that challenging because they have not yet made the shift. They will, however, continue their journey with others learning what they intended before incarnation, in the way and time they choose.

The ebb and flow of life is reflected by our emotions, yet our frequency remains stable. Our frequency is our soul's energy.

My frequency supported me through this time with a stability of knowing life is a process for everyone. It showed me how my life is expanding and that as I change, things around me change. As I love myself more fully, the people I choose to be around in my life reflect this and value me for who I am. There is a balance between loving unconditionally and choosing environments that nurture us. In fact, these are both possible to achieve simultaneously. That can manifest by loving ourselves so fully that we can love another while not needing to share their life. It's all about, *what is for the highest good of all*. Love doesn't harbour conditions, it just is.

As we look around the world or even in your own life, using the worldwide pandemic as an example, we can see how the feeling of fear, and confusion controls people. For most of us, the separation this event caused was extremely painful. We saw more loneliness, mental health issues, self-harm, division of family and friends and an increase of addictive substances flood our planet. Fear creates barriers that inhibit unity.

Our ego mind has been taught to run our lives and control as much as possible for fear of not being right and not being safe. Fearfulness and the need for self-protection have led us to being resistant to gentle signs from the universe. Signs for change or confirmation of direction, which has blocked us from noticing the wisdom that we are a part of.

Up until now, change has been the result of a big wake-up call, often shocking the person or population awake. It's not the pain that destroys us; it's the things we do to avoid the pain. There are many platforms of running away from pain. Such as addictions, blaming others, self-harm, killing, disconnecting from yourself through some forms of mental illness, blocking feelings through pharmaceuticals, having affairs, taking illegal drugs, avoidance of taking responsibility or simply shutting down emotionally. Then there's over eating, smoking/vaping, compulsive spending, gambling and all the other activities that humans engage in to avoid feeling pain. This perpetuates more of what has been causing havoc on this planet. We have been conditioned to think pain is something wrong and we have to fix it, rather than it being information. When we really feel the effects of what we have done or been through, it serves as a reason to make a change.

We just need to look back in history to see the events that occurred before we were willing to implement change, which comes about by feeling the pain of our actions or experiences. For example: With the killing of George Floyd by the US police officer in May 2020, the "Black Lives Matter" movement began. The depletion of some whale species to near extinction led to the banning of whaling in many countries by 1969 and to international cessation of whaling as an industry in the late 1980's. Excessive impact on fauna, killing thousands of cetaceans: dolphins, whales and porpoises as well as turtles, sharks and other species. In 1989 Greenpeace campaigned to end the use of deadly drift nets. This led to a worldwide ban in 1992. However, in all of these cases problems still occur and some people ignore the need for change. These are the people who have yet to feel the harm and the horrific pain, these activities are causing.

The more willing we are, to fully feel and truthfully see what is happening, the more we are inclined to make changes. We have seen this through our own lifetime, and everything is pointing to it happening again, the same but different. Whether that change will be personal, local or collective will be the individual's Fate or Destiny. Fate is a learning path, we grow through our past challenges and Destiny is a path of love, we experience in the moment for loves sake. We begin with the path of Fate. One path must be finished before the other one can begin.

Our 3D ego developed to help us navigate certain 3D environments and terrains. It is not equipped for the spiritual journey, which is why it usually resists the path in the initial stages. A 3D ego can be defensive, avoidant, afraid, doubting, aggressive, in denial and so on. The spiritual journey over time becomes a great fire that begins to transform the ego into an ally. In this fire after the resistant phase, the ego may start to relax as it realises that meditation and other spiritual practices are actually not dangerous.

Beyond the relaxing phase comes the transformational phase where negative qualities are gradually burnt away to reveal golden new ones such as confidence, courage, determination, focus, optimism, resilience, resourcefulness, self-discipline, tenacity and more. The ego was never designed to be the master of our destiny. The spiritual journey reveals the true master of our destiny, which is our higher-selves.

Most of our lives have involved experiences offering us opportunities for growth. Growth takes embracing the courage to allow yourself to break. If you feel an experience and fear it will break you, then break. Let spirit crack you open; I have surrendered to this many times in my own life. When your child whom you love with every ounce of your being, chooses to blame you for their issues rather than do personal work and projects their unresolved pain onto you. Let your soul be forged by the agony of illusion, that which you are not. When the ego is going through the fire or "the dark night of the soul", you have, or will, find these are changes for your highest good. Let these experiences transform you into the most perfect instrument of destiny. As I walked through that fire and released some final attachments, I have come out a much stronger and more authentic version of myself. As difficult as it was at the time, I am grateful for this experience and know it serves us all in some way. The change I've noticed is- I'm no longer taking responsibility for making others feel comfortable. I have done that up until this time, even if it was at a cost to me. And finally, I'm comfortable with others not understanding my journey. Thank you, life school.

Just this morning I took a workshop poster into my yoga school. I recently met an amazing business coach and creative ideas artist. We were planning to run a "Playshop for soul led Entrepreneurs" on the premises in a month's time. I'm not sure but the poster may not have fitted the criteria for the noticeboard and when I asked for it to be displayed the owner looked a little hesitant, a tiny look, nothing most people would even notice. Being sensitive I picked up this subtle response, she was very busy and it may have been bad timing on my part. She said OK, I'll put it up. Now the old me would have said anything to have her feel more comfortable, even if it meant me not displaying the poster. This time, I just noticed this option but wasn't compelled to say anything. I decided to let her do what she feels to do and go with that. It became obvious that what I had done, with setting boundaries and valuing myself, had grounded into a shift in behaviours. Those challenging experiences with my relationships have readied me for my next chapter.

The people I know who are awake have come to this conscious awareness through challenging times. I have myself, even though at times I've resisted my life's path.

If you can embrace the fullness of your pain, you can embrace the fullness of your power.

Challenges which we often resist or judge as wrong actually guide us to our healing path, calling us to go deeper than we would choose to go. Another blessing from experiencing challenges is that it can bring us together, unify us as we reach out for help.

It takes great courage to let go again and again, especially if we've made choices and created a life from the wounded parts of ourselves. As you do the work, those choices no longer fit. Death feeds life. Whatever you let go of is making space to nourish and generate the next chapter of your life that wants to birth through you. It doesn't matter how old you are, you have the power to alter your destiny. It may have some very challenging moments but remember life is about the choices you make. Choose to know that you can do hard things, and how often do hard things lead to great rewards?

I have a personal story about the universe wanting to guide me in a new direction. When I was working at Lifeline (a crisis telephone support line), I was doing work that I thoroughly enjoyed. I held a few positions in the office; supervisor, trainer, volunteer, roster person and cleaner. I had started my Clinical Hypnotherapy practice but was only seeing a couple of clients on a part-time basis.

Each person is at their own place in the evolution of their soul. Some are currently allowing fear to control them to a larger degree than others, as most of us have at some point in our evolution. One such person worked in the office with me, a place where I worked for close to five years. She seemed to be consistently unhappy, complaining and fearful, particularly focusing on me.

The more fearful a person is, the more difficult it seems for them to be around the light or those of us who are shifting our frequency. At that time, I wasn't aware of how my frequency affected others. It's their resistance that makes it difficult. I wonder if you have experienced any of this in your own life? I was happy working in this place, in fact I loved most of my time there. Something had to disrupt my comfort to move me on because on reflection, I was no longer growing and would have stayed there indefinitely. Our life's path that we planned prior to our incarnation will guide us to the new road, when it's time to move and grow. But if we don't surrender to it, we will be forced. It's a matter of taking the step or being pushed.

It became increasingly difficult for me to stay in this work environment; I was struggling to be around the energy of this person, which was a daily challenge, not to mention the effect this disharmony was having on my wellbeing. When a sensitive person is around others that project negatively towards them, over a period of time it can cause physical, even emotional disease. We feel everything deeply and negative thoughts create negative energy and it's unhealthy at every level. This reflected my wounded selves, as yet unhealed.

I finally found the courage and gave one month's notice, so with the support of management we could train someone to replace me. During that time one of the volunteers came to me and said, "You should meet with a friend of mine, who has a space to rent in a healing centre that might just be perfect for you". And as life would have it, another event got my attention, just to confirm it was time for me to move on. One week after I gave notice, my landlord put my house rent up by one hundred Australian dollars a week. That was a significant rise at the time, especially considering I was working at a charity, and they are unable to pay high wages, which added to my reason for having so many roles in the office. There was a jump in the value of properties and the owner of my house was a solicitor. He assured me, the house value had increased greatly, and the rent was reflecting this, so I knew I had to accept that. At that time this amount was impossible for me to pay, and I knew I had to move. In the perfection of the universe, when I look back, I wouldn't have been able to create this new life ahead of me from that town and that house.

With my youngest child still living at home as well as not having a guaranteed income, I surrendered to the universe to guide me.

If you are experiencing uncertainty in your life as I was then, I would like to introduce a concept that I refer to as "The power of the pause". I don't own this idea but it's one of the gems my life has shown me over time, and it's a great support during these unsure times. When we allow things to play out before making hasty moves, you will find certainty and in time even clarity. Wait until you feel sure, if you're unsure do nothing. Once you go through the power of the storm with all the events ebbing and flowing, there will come a moment in time when you find certainty, and then your body will let you know by feeling a sense of calmness, that you are ready.

The universe asked me to step into the unknown empty handed and has continued to do so many times since then. Long story short, this was the beginning of my current business and practice, *Hygea Counselling Services*. The name Hygea came from a spiritual healer I saw many years earlier who told me she kept hearing the word Hygea as I laid on her table. I decided to research it at the local library and found it was a Greek word meaning, "Goddess of Health" so I kept it in mind, not knowing why. I have been successfully working full time in my practice since 2009. I consistently surrender to my life's path, to where it leads me. This is usually not an easy decision, and it almost always takes a decent amount of courage. Yet this way of life has strengthened me and my trust in myself, Spirit, the Divine and the design of the universe. I've been asked to surrender into my life's path several times since then and maybe this book is another change in direction for my life. I guess time will tell and life will show me.

Each time our path leads us in a new direction it can seem a bit scary in the beginning. The 3D ego's model of needing to be in control of everything, now seems like many lifetimes ago. My life has taught me to trust that the universe, the Divine, my higher-self and life's path is leading me to the destiny of my highest good and greatest joy, as it is for you and all of us. The only way we can make it a struggle is if we hold onto resistance. And if it's for my highest good, it's for the highest good of all because essentially, we are all one.

One type of sensitive HSP is what is commonly known as a "Wounded Healer". This is an example of a life of challenges that prepares the person for their mission. It teaches them empathy, to feel deeply and understand other people's challenges and how to face fear and darkness so they can then be there for others in their struggle.

Many awakened people who are practising healing of some sort fall into this category of "Wounded Healers". When a soul has traversed through their darkest times and faced it all, they become unafraid of the dark side of planet earth. Because they have sat with their own pain they can sit with other people's. This might explain why you have maybe traversed through so much darkness in your own life.

Many HSP's are also Star-Seeds, Light-workers or possibly one of a number of other types of beings that have a different heritage/history to human beings, they/you/we come from other planets/ galaxies/worlds.

INCONVENIENT CONSCIOUSNESS

You may have struggled with challenging childhoods, experiences, relationships and struggled to fit in or be understood. That is because you are not meant to fit in, your purpose was never to fit in because you are not a part of the collective. *We don't want to fit into something we came here to change.*

This journey is designed to go easier on new souls, so know if you are having, or have, had challenges it's because your heart is brave, and you have chosen to grow through experience and perhaps even cut the path for others. You can do it, because love is what heals. You are answering your soul's call to keep your heart open, even when it has been broken or feels like it's been trampled on. Keeping your heart open is brave because this is how you feel everything. It also allows you to shine your light and demonstrate by example how to live from the heart. Don't worry that you don't fit in, or that sometimes you struggle to understand or manage human behaviour.

That's simply a reminder of who you are, fear is something we have all tasted so we understand it yet it remains foreign to the hearts of lightworkers. Fear shuts people's hearts and does awful things to you and to others because we become disconnected from our feelings. That's what closing your heart is about. When the heart is closed all negative emotions implode. It's not personal, it's just fear. This phenomenon is foreign to you and has broken your heart many, many times. Your heart is so big and brave it has the courage to offer love even where there has been hurt and pain projected on you.

This heaviness is coming to an end as you are learning what is good for you, what supports your energy. In that process you are discovering what is more helpful than any other activity. It is getting to know who you really are. It is the main focus of evolution and will help everything fall into place. It seems like a simple thing and that maybe we should already know this but there is more to discover than you can ever imagine.

The soul is sovereign and never needs healing. It is our essence and the eternal aspect of us humans. Everything else, except for love, is a fleeting experience. This is a time that many of us are being activated to move into a Stewardship of supporting our soul and that of humanity. This is an axis point of moving from only valuing the physical, toward valuing soul and aligning our personality with our soul.

My intention in talking about this waking-up process is to offer, to those of you who are ready, a new perspective and perhaps with this, some new tools, even some motivation and passion and, ideally, an opportunity to prepare for change.

Waking up, in essence is waking up to who you are and what your place is in the universe. Lacking direction, passion, motivation or confidence can be signs that you are not as self-aware as you might think. Self-awareness opens up further still and becomes clear when you are aligned to your purpose, your higher-self, your soul. Just like your sensitivity, your purpose is closely connected to who you are. It is an expression of your passion and your essence.

In order to know your purpose, you must know who you are. How can you know what your passion is if you don't know who you are? For example, HSP who are also healers are usually drawn to a therapeutic, caring, healing area of work. HSP who are creative people, will find a creative expression which could also serve as healing in whatever area they feel drawn to. For example, I know a HSP who is also very creative, and she practices art therapy for children. Waking up leads you to living authentically and it also allows you to find and embody your purpose.

Highly Sensitive People (HSP) are the subject of this chapter, and this leads us into other areas of life other than our physical existence because we are not just one thing.

All of us have many interesting and different aspects that make up our unique and individual self.

The sum of our experiences and what we have done with them, as well as the universal spark within or the essence of us, are the hands that have moulded this human experience at this time and in this place.

There are no two people or souls that are exactly the same, anywhere in the universe. To me that is extraordinary. Only you can do what you came here to do in your unique way. In some ways, HSP are ahead of their time because even if a large chunk of the world is sleeping while playing out a belief in separation, we live our life in oneness through knowing how it feels to be not only ourselves but another person. We demonstrate this by feeling what other people feel, by finding empathy a natural part of our perceptions.

As we release the old and step into our true-self, our focus is balanced both on our own lives and those of others. This is an innate behaviour for us. Many of us get the message when another is in need as though our thinking has expanded to universal thought. As I write these words, they seem new to me: "Universal thought". It may not be a new concept to some, but it seems to me that being a universal person, which is the evolution of humanity and the purpose of the shift, would then lead us to experiencing universal thought.

As I go through my day, people just pop into my mind, my awareness has expanded from this small personal life. I wonder if that is the magic of the connectedness I feel, a part of who I am, who we all are in our natural state? It would appear that this is where the new earth is leading those of us who are making the journey to unity and love. Not only are we letting go of fear and limitation, but our everyday thinking is becoming more global. I am very excited by the endless possibilities for our planet and our human family and am *hopeful* that each of us will find and traverse on our path of least resistance.

Hope is a word that can be seen as being passive and lacking power, so I want to talk about it a little more. The level of hope is an indicator of the level of love within you, it can be used as a personal gauge to check-in with. How hopeful am I? How loving am I? You can actually use it as a measuring system Hope 0% = Love 0%. Hope is an agent of change, and it is the super hero within us showing up. Hope is the steering wheel of life. With hope we can imagine turning our steering wheel where we want to go. In a new direction. Hope takes courage as we imagine a different reality from what we have been conditioned to believe and what is currently all around us. I see it as a warrior's emotion.

There really is a lot to explore in this subject of Highly Sensitive People as I trust you've become more aware of. These people vary just like any other type of person, but they all have great empathy and compassion. Often, depending on their level of acceptance and understanding of themselves which brings balance, they demonstrate other gifts. Such as high levels of intuition, healing abilities, creative abilities and those innate attributes that free or awaken human's share, not only for themselves but for all of humanity. Perhaps these are the results of our lifetimes of experience, before this life.

It can be a challenging path to be highly sensitive, I'm sure it was in the past when we look at the history of our planet, just as it is in the current state of the world. It can take great courage, but I want to acknowledge you right here, right now, as a warrior of the light and a bringer of change to our planet. So please, no matter what trials or resistance you come up against and, no doubt you will, never stop being your wonderful sensitive self. This planet needs you. Be true to yourself without apologies and the journey will open up with more ease and flow than you could even imagine or that you might have experienced up until now.

We HSP are a living example of how things can be in our new world. We are the path cutters, the way showers, the courageous women, men, children and all humans who are, with every beat of our heart, creating a new road map of possibility for our planet and its people. We are a living example of the heart of creation reminding everyone who *crosses* our path, that we are all connected, and that love is our very essence. We are a reminder that we are love and we can only truly be happy and live the life of our dreams when we return to that.

I sincerely hope this chapter has offered you the exploration that it offered me in its writing. To uncover more about who you really are and why you are here at this auspicious time.

CHAPTER 5 QUESTIONS:

A) Can you identify a limiting or fear-based belief that is holding you back from being all of who you are?

B) Are you an HSP (highly sensitive person) or do you know someone who is? What makes that clear to you?

C) What part of this information is helpful to you and why?

D) How much do you fully accept and own this HSP aspect of yourself/themselves in your everyday life, even when it's inconvenient or embarrassing? If you want to accept this at a deeper level, how will you do that?

E) What are your struggles as a HSP or sharing your life with such a person? What are some of the gifts?

F) Are you in resistance or willing to surrender to your life's path?

G) Knowing that where you are is perfect for your path, where do you see yourself on the journey of knowing yourself? E.g.: Not yet started, the beginning: up to 25%, the middle: up to 50% or well along: up to 75%+? Are you content with that?

H) Have you faced your shadow or any aspect of it? If so, what changed?

I) Do you have clarity with what your purpose is?

J) How does fear limit your life?

K) Do you communicate with spirit and/or meditate, or would you like to?

L) How do you understand Fate and Destiny?

CHAPTER 6

SHIFTING DIMENSIONS; EMBODYING SOUL.

There is a new world being birthed- the Fifth Dimension or 5D. As for most births, it can be a bit messy. Birth of the new calls for a releasing or letting go of the old. As mentioned previously, in our current reality the intention of large corporations and business, banking and financial systems, education systems, many religions, and all levels of governments, the legal system and much of the health systems of the world are about profit and are ready for an overhaul/upgrade and many of them, a complete reset. The problems resulting from an environment that cares more about profit than people, are showing up in almost every sector of our lives. They are not aligned to our new world. We are living in times of change, extraordinary change and where we are moving to is largely new territory, but one thing is for certain, it is for the highest good of all.

Change can trigger fear in people, especially if we are holding onto control which is just a form of fear. When we view this shift from a higher perspective, it helps us see there really is nothing to fear. There are many layers and levels of change that are presenting themselves from the foundations of society to planetary shifts, to the conscious inner work that many of us have said yes to.

INCONVENIENT CONSCIOUSNESS

This shift of consciousness has been planned for eons of time and is supported by many souls who have come to this planet for this very purpose. The souls who have come here are best explained in waves, not the same as the first wavers I mentioned earlier, this is different because it's a time related thing. These people have a similar purpose to the first, second and third wavers, by being here to support all beings and the planet herself.

There are generational waves of support, and each wave has its unique role in developing the New Earth. It can be reassuring to know there is a divine plan in motion and each of these souls have a piece of the jigsaw puzzle. They have incarnated into a human body to be here at this time: the Star-Seeds, the Blue Rays, the Indigos, the Lightworkers and the Earth Angels are all a part of this generational wave movement. This will happen in waves; each wave or generation has a timing to wake up and step up to their mission. It is not about one being better or more advanced than another, it is simply the way it works.

There is a lot of work to be done in many areas of life and my feeling is it will take around 20 years to fully put these changes into place. When we consider we are building a New World, 20 years seems reasonable to me but, like everything, this will be affected by free-will.

We have all the support we need to get the job done, including the councils of light. In fact, the entire universe is supporting this shift in consciousness that is referred to as the Ascension. The council of light is a team of ascended masters, light beings, angels, and guides devoted to the rising of Earth and all of humanity. They are a team of benevolent beings who are here to assist in the raising of consciousness on the planet. This is why waking up is so crucial, so we can see and sense more than has been commonly accepted. Many of you reading this book are a part of this group of souls who came here at this time with a bigger mission than you might have realised. These benevolent beings are here to help achieve your soul's mission and are guiding you every step of the way. The more awake you are, the more you will become aware of this.

Many people have been working in an industry that they thought they loved and would move forward in, only to discover things didn't go to plan. This is often a sign that this is the area you came here to help change but you needed to understand how it is broken first so you can, at the right time, bring in your ideas and new ways that support unity, equality, respect and love.

However, we live in a world where freewill reigns. All beings, whether they are your Spirit-Guides, Angels, or Higher-Self, they require your permission before they can assist you. If you would like assistance, it's time to ask. You can do that in speaking out loud, in a prayer, in a meditative state, however you choose. Perhaps you will ask to be shown a sign that helps you remember your mission? Perhaps you will pick up a crayon and start drawing or free writing?

When we drop into our creative self it gives the universe space to connect with us. Signs are another tool of consciousness. I find asking for signs and then noticing them is a great reminder that I am not alone and that I am being supported on my journey. Signs can be- feathers, coins, literal signs, lyrics to a song or anything that gets your attention. You can even ask for them to be specific and really obvious, as I have, if you feel you might miss them.

I remember talking to a close friend on the phone while she was living overseas. She was finding a few things challenging at the time, living in a new country, with such a different culture and away from her family and friends. We often spoke on a conscious level about such things as signs, so I asked her if she had been given any signs to help guide her or let her know she is not alone. She answered, "No, I have asked but I haven't received any." Then almost out of the blue she added, "Wow, the beautiful bridge I'm looking at is covered in graffiti, that's a shame." I asked her, "What does it say?" She answered, "The answer you are looking for is inside you." We both burst out laughing because there it was, larger than life, the sign she had asked for. It can be easy to miss them if we are stuck in our head with thoughts of doubt and fear, but they will be there. All you need to do is ask and trust.

The entire universe is consistently in a process of change and because of our oneness, everything effects everything else. This evolutionary shift (the Ascension) is predestined and before we incarnated, we were both chosen for this role and we agreed to it in its entirety. It is leading us to creating Heaven on Earth and in divine timing, to enjoy living the life of our dreams.

The ego personality part of us is conditioned to feel safer when things stay the same so we feel in control. Opposed to things changing and calling on us to surrender and trust in the plan of our life. This desire for things to remain the same is true even if the things are not working. This is one of the reasons why, when an organisation wants to change things, they usually introduce the change slowly, often almost unnoticeable. That is unless they are using fear to produce a rapid change or a certain view that has an underlying agenda. Waking up makes these two differences more obvious. It takes courage to see things as they really are and not as we prefer them to be.

The dark side of our planet can be quite confronting but denying it, only perpetuates it. This is a form of agreement. If fear is a part of your psyche, then facing the truth or waking up will allow you to identify and address it. We can only improve those things that we identify as needing reform.

It's often the slow gradual changes that can go unnoticed especially to those people who are asleep. When change is being presented ask yourself the question, "Who is gaining from this change?" Even more valid, "How do you feel about it?" Remember we don't need to get distracted by the back story or going down any rabbit holes or judging people or events; we are just wanting to see things as they really are so we can support a change.

So as long as you know yourself, where you stand and who is directing your life, they are the main goals. In this currently reality if it's not in everyone's best interest, you can be assured someone is gaining control and/or making money from it. Money and control are food for the fearful ego, our shadow or small self. When anything is for the greater good, we as a collective are free to discuss it and share our knowledge therefore, everyone gains from it.

Most of the business world decided a long time ago that the share-holder's profit is more important than the care and service of people.

For business models based on profit alone, not even the health of the planet that supports our very life comes into consideration. When profits are the number one focus, this is separation culture and fast becoming the old way of doing business. An "us" against "them" mentality, and the view that only the wellbeing of the people in charge and the company's profit really matters.

Those structures that are not in alignment with the highest good, I believe, over the years ahead they will be adjusted or will crumble and be replaced by heart-centred businesses. Where care of each other and service is the main focus and value that is upheld.

This New World that is the result of our Ascension is founded in unity, love, equality, health and well-being, abundance and joy for every single one of us, including our animal friends and nature.

This wake-up is an opportunity call to everyone who chooses to leave this experience of struggle and separation behind and to follow our lives path to the New World. Some people will choose not to do this so will either play out their 3D life and then pass over or leave this current life time prematurely through physical death. And reincarnate to continue their third dimensional or karmic experience in an environment for that experience. While those of us who choose this shift will make the commitment to do the work and experience a reality shift while still in our bodies. How amazing we are, doing something never done before with no roadmap. We are on the adventure of our lifetimes.

Our life is leading us to this new reality and only our free will resistance can hinder the journey or delay us. This shift won't be a choice everyone makes at this time, but I feel it's as inevitable as the evolution of creation. Change is inevitable, just the timing is our choice.

To understand resistance can be helpful, as it can often be unconscious, in other words something that's out of our conscious awareness. It shows up as fear in the form of protection, where our unconscious mind will hold onto an old belief, an addiction or a story that you formed a long time ago and makes the current events match that old pattern. Resistance cannot continue without a secondary gain. As for my example earlier, I resisted the change because my mind thought I was safer with the old behaviour. It took trust to surrender in where my life was leading me to release the resistance and we can all do that if we choose to.

IORINA

You may have heard about or experienced some physical changes or symptoms as we traverse through this shift, this process of ascension. It is affecting us on every level. The body is transitioning from carbon to crystalline in order to hold more light. You may often feel tired or less energetic as this change takes energy to move to a higher state of being. Additionally, this fatigue may not be consistent, you might find your energy levels fluctuate throughout the day. At times you could feel a burst of energy followed by feelings of intense tiredness. Your body is learning to balance and harmonise with the new crystalline structure, and this can take time. The fatigue is the result of energetic changes and adjustments rather than physical activity. As you transition into a crystalline based body, mood swings and irritability are common signs of this process. The transformation into a crystalline based body involves significant energetic shifts. Your body is adjusting to higher frequencies and integrating more light which can disrupt your emotional balance. These emotional fluctuations can be challenging to manage but understanding their cause, will help you navigate with more ease and compassion.

As your body releases old energies and patterns, you may find yourself revisiting past emotions and trauma. This release is necessary for your transformation. You might feel overwhelmed by emotions that seem to come out of nowhere. Remember there is support available, perhaps professionally or you may enrol a trusted friend. This is your body's way of clearing out the old to make room for the new.

During the transition to a crystalline based body, you might find it increasingly difficult to concentrate and focus. This can be particularly frustrating if you are used to having sharp mental clarity and a strong attention span. This lack of focus is a natural part of your body integrating higher frequencies and more light. Your mind is also adapting to these changes. The shift can seem to create a sense of mental fog where thoughts seem scattered and its challenging to maintain a steady train of thought. Your brain is learning to operate at a higher level of consciousness which can temporarily disrupt your usual cognitive functions. This difficulty concentrating can manifest in various ways. You might start a task to find yourself easily distracted or you could struggle to remember things, you usually remember easily. It can feel like a haze on your mental landscape.

These changes are at a cellular level so will present many symptoms. Headaches are due to your brain adjusting to new energy patterns, body aches, stiffness, soreness in muscles and joints even without engaging in exercise. This is because your body is releasing old dense energies and making room for a new, lighter, crystalline structure. Digestive issues are also common, your digestive system is particularly sensitive to energetic changes.

You might experience bloating, changes in appetite, digestive disturbances, these are your body's way of purging toxins and old energies. You are integrating energies of the new crystalline form. It is essential you listen to your body and adjust your diet to suit, opting for lighter, nutrient rich foods. This shift in our physical body often brings a higher sense of emotional intensity and sensitivity. This can feel overwhelming as your emotional body aligns with higher vibrational energies. You might find your emotions are intense; feeling sadness, anger, joy or love and it might take you by surprise with their depth and power. This is your body's way of releasing old emotional patterns and making room for new frequencies of energies. And you might become more emotionally connected to the feelings of people around you, even if you have been detached in the past. This can be a blessing and a challenge energetically as you learn to manage your emotional boundaries more carefully. This can also bring past traumas, supressed feelings, old emotions to the surface and they can arise unexpectedly seeking acknowledgement and release.

Increases in your intuitive and psychic abilities such as your clairvoyance, clairaudience, clairsentience is a direct result of your evolving energetic structure, allowing you to access higher realms of information. You might experience a clearer sense of what is right for you and what is not, decisions that once took a long time now happen effortlessly. This is your body aligning to higher frequencies enabling you to navigate your path with greater clarity and confidence.

An example I offer for this is a decision I made not to attend a special occasion that someone very close to me was running. It was as though my body had developed an alignment that was not allowing me to put myself in an energy that was less than I deserved and that I had accepted in the past. This was happening while my love for them had not changed. It seemed more like the love and value of myself was what had changed. It had risen in frequency. It felt like my head was playing catch up, making excuses why I should do what I've always done.

It felt like one of the most difficult things I have ever done. The level of challenge helped me to know this was a significant event and was making room for my new path to open up. These shifts are not easy or even comfortable but that is not a reason to revert back to the old ways. In time everything will fall into a new place, a more loving and empowering place, not just for myself but for everyone. As we trust in the process and reach out for help, our soul's plan unfolds. If something you thought was for you doesn't work out, know there is something better awaiting you.

Sleep patterns may also be disrupted, and this is a natural part of the process as your body and mind adjust to higher frequencies of a new energy structure. You can also feel a detachment from the physical world. This signals a shift in your consciousness and perception. This can manifest in different ways perhaps you find yourself less interested in material pursuits and more drawn to spiritual or metaphysical topics. Things like hobbies, pursuits, even work may no longer hold the same appeal. You might find a stronger pull towards introspection and meditation and exploring the deeper aspects of existence. Remember, all of these symptoms are temporary and are leading you to freedom and expansion.

Once we begin to awaken, new choices present themselves to us. Our choices often open up as we choose to surrender to our life's path.

Here's an example of this: I spent time in a spiritual group, this was the time I spent mostly away from my children when they lived with their dad. I saw a person who interpreted readings just before the inception of this chapter. The message was that my life was changing and I was being asked by spirit to step into the unknown empty handed. This would take me on a journey of self-discovery that would lead me to finding clarity, and direction for a bigger picture. The message was "Your children will be in good hands with their dad as this time is fated for everyone involved." Now I wouldn't advise or agree it's a good idea to make decisions based on another's opinion yet I had already felt these things, and, to me, it was more of a confirmation than anything.

In this group I experienced communication from beings of other dimensions. This experience felt so genuine and reassured me this was a benevolent group. This experience caused me to start questioning the rest of life. It felt authentic and sacred and I know this is not something that can be faked. The most impactful part of this event was as I was listening to the guidance, the information coming through, the entire room lit-up with the brightest white light that I had ever experienced. It wasn't a physical light as I had my eyes closed, it was esoteric. In fact, I had never experienced anything like this before, it felt other worldly, and it took my breath away. If I could give it a name, I would call it love. It felt like a spiritual sign, a loving presence, not at all earthly and it was totally organic. In that moment I felt that I was where I was meant to be. After knowing that my children were settled with their dad, unaware of the challenges yet to unfold, we were all on a journey. Our collective journey of letting go had begun.

I began working on letting go of the attachments and judgements from myself and others. In particular, not having my children live with me and what people thought of me. I was letting go of needing approval from friends and family, who didn't understand our choices. This was a decision that felt difficult from the start. I let go of most of my earthly possessions and that was a bit daunting. I kept a few personal treasures, photo albums (our main way of keeping memories back then) a few pieces of furniture and some clothes. I was totally surrendered to what was in front of me, without knowing exactly what that was. I did have fears and all of my limited beliefs and patterns still active, but somehow, I knew this was for me.

I moved from my home town to live with this group of strangers, (except for my friend who introduced me) to a little riverside town. It was a small town, without distractions. Its simplicity was perfect for the work we were about to take on. At this time there were only a few shops in the main street and a beautiful river to enjoy.

In this community we shared everything and lived as much as possible with love as our foundation. We were truly cutting a path, there was no road map for us, we made it up as we went. It felt a bit like jumping into the void because it went against our collective conditioning of finding safety from people and objects outside of ourselves. One of the most valuable gifts I received from this group was learning how to let go of my ego's attachments and all the things that I thought I was, so that I could begin to embrace and be who I really am.

The ego builds identities that make it feel in control and important. I *thought* that I believed these things about myself, at least on the outside: I was a caring mother, a good daughter, an independent woman, a person who paid her bills on time, someone who always did her best, told her children that they were loved, and an independent thinker. I was aware I was looking for outside approval and maybe there were more fears and hidden wounds than I had realised. I saw myself as the person I had made up from my unknown wounding. Yet underneath it all I had feelings of unworthiness, even hopelessness when I let myself feel it. There was a part of me that I didn't give a voice to back then, that in my darkest nights wondered if there was more to me, more to this life? Not devaluing my role as a mother at all, but being honest and accepting the inner fire to become more of who I am.

My list was made up of the story I told myself about myself, to make myself feel worthy. I discovered I was none of these things, these where just things I did, and these attachments stopped me from discovering who I really am. It's not the things or activities themselves that are the issue; it's the attachment to them. Hanging onto something that I used as a part of my identity got in the way of finding out who I really am.

Following my life's path consciously, as I was endeavouring to do at this time, included and still includes, going with the flow of change. Nothing in the universe stays the same and our lives are no different. When it came time to leave this group, it was something we had to do alone and without any support as the group philosophy was to stay, regardless. I had sold my car, stored my essential furniture, beloved photo albums and a few treasures to experience this way of life. I was going into the unknown empty handed. Everything I was taking with me fitted in a couple of large suit cases and my bank account had just a few hundred dollars in it. My thoughts at the time were still of fear of survival but beneath that there was something urging me forward.

I had done what felt like enormous amounts of inner work just to make this move but because of the time on the planet, there was still plenty to clear. I somehow pushed past my fears and listened to my inner guidance system of feeling. It was time for the next step, without even knowing what that was. On reflection, this showed me that my trust in the Divine has always been unwavering.

It feels innate to trust in my heart. The heart thrives on the unknown and it isn't always logical or even reasonable, but it does know the path of least resistance to finding our way home to wholeness. This is a feeling like "I know what I have to do and maybe a couple of the steps, but I don't know exactly where the heart is leading me". It was beginning to feel like something I could trust beyond the fear.

The missing steps always reveal themselves when we surrender and trust. I know I might make a few wrong turns along the way but somehow, I know things will work out eventually. Even mistakes have great gifts to offer us, including humility. On this path of surrender you will see some people leave your life, as each of your paths go their own way. These seem like predestined events.

As you journey through life you will be drawn to many like-minded people, some who have made contracts with you to meet up at this stage of your journey to move forward with you. They may offer friendship, learnings, support or guidance as you may do for them too and this can be for a short or long time.

The heart is not logical but from your heart strings your soul tribe will be pulled to you. Some of these people are here to work with you on your mission, some are to have fun with, and some are your soul family. When we live untethered, our creativity expands, we enjoy playfulness, gratitude and curiosity. Brilliant ideas will come to you as well as those seen and unseen beings who support your journey. As you are willing to surrender and trust, miracles happen more frequently.

My inner guidance who I now know as my spirit guides, told me it was time to leave. Things began to feel a bit off is the best way I can describe it. My sense of this time was that this experience had run its course. I chose to change my focus and withdraw my energy from this group and life. A friend of mine was in and out of this group but never fully committed. Although many people struggled to see what we were really about, he seemed to understand our intentions even though it wasn't for him.

We tended to trigger fear in many of the people in our lives, as love tends to do. It's fair to say in that time on the planet, our choices and way of life was most unusual and most of our family and friends would either project their fears, judge or run from us.

My friend understood more than most people, what we were about and that our intentions were loving, so he felt like someone I could go to. He rented a place that he wasn't using in Noosa Heads, which is a beautiful seaside town in Queensland, and a lot further north from where I was living. My plan was to fly there because I had just enough money for airfare and some food. I hoped on my arrival I would find some work to help me return to my home town, where my children and family were living. My original town had little public transport for work access, which I would have to rely on until I was able to buy a car.

I got up early the day after I arrived in this peaceful little town with one thought on my mind; I must find a job and save some money to get back home. I could only bring with me whatever I could carry in a bag so was limited with my choice of attire for job hunting. I was surprised to notice that there were more than twenty real estate agents in the main street of Noosa. Anyone would think, at least I did, that must mean this was a thriving industry and there was a chance I could find work there.

My first stop was at the beginning of the street, I went in and asked if there was any work? I was told, "If I hadn't sold real estate previously, I had no chance of finding work in this town, especially in Hastings Street". "This main street", I was told, "was where the cream of the crop in real estate worked". I walked on, and office after office said more or less the same thing, "no", "no" and "no".

That night as I sat in my friends rented unit with nothing but the bag, I carried with me and reflected on my day. The shift that occurs when we surrender to life can look unreasonable to outsiders and I still had work to do in this area but fortunately I was advanced enough to trust that I would be ok. Or perhaps it was that I had just enough hope to keep going.

There was a calling, a sense that is difficult to put into words other than to say it felt like intuition and it was speaking to me. This inner sense drew my attention to the first office I approached for work. It was nudging me to explore the possibility that I just might find work there. Another possible thread in the unwoven tapestry of my new life.

The second day in my new town, I went back to the first office. I asked to see the principal again. Even though I was feeling a little unsure and out of my depth when he appeared, I explained that even though he had said no, I had a sense he might have some work for me. He was quite surprised and after his initial shock said, "I like your tenacity and I want to introduce you to my wife because she makes all the decisions when hiring staff." After that meeting, they offered me a job on one condition, that I did a real estate agent training course in Melbourne the following week. I agreed to their condition even though I didn't know how any of that was possible.

I followed my inner guidance and watched as miracles unfolded. Without having an income, the bank gave me a credit card for the exact amount I needed to fly to Melbourne, cover accommodation for the week and so off I went. When we're in the stream of life, trusting the process everything flows, have you noticed that?

It may not be what we expect or even what we prefer but it's like being in a slip stream, everything flows easily. I just kept dealing with what was in front of me. I stayed up studying each night and completed the exam with half an hour to spare but I had a feeling I did ok.

On my return my new boss called me into her office and congratulated me for coming in top of the class. She told me I could start work the following week. She showed me the local paper and much to my surprise, I was on the front page. The heading read, "Expert real estate agent for Sunrise beach". Unbeknownst to her, I didn't even know where this lovely sounding suburb was. As most people know, it's tricky to sell properties without a car so that was my next hurdle. I was guided by my friend who referred me to a car dealership that offered the option of renting a car weekly. I was paid a retainer which was just bread and butter money, but it covered the car, a small one-bedroom flat with a mattress on the floor, fridge, table and chair.

Life really taught me that there really is no need to force anything, to hold on tightly or to fear our life's path. It is designed perfectly for each of us, to understand what we came here to learn and to be who we came here to be. This example above called on my courage to let go and trust, putting into practice and grounding the things I had learnt while in the spiritual group. These strengths are now in my storehouse of resources to access as I need. Contrary to what we have be conditioned to believe, we are never alone, and the Universe is compassionate and wise. It has our back. And when we know this, our frequency matches it and we attract it.

The Buddha said, "Craving or Attachments are the root of all suffering". Attachments are a natural part of the human psyche but when they become too tight, they cause fear, they also cause all the negative thoughts and restrictive feelings related to fear. Being attached keeps us stuck and so our life will show us this by creating struggles. Life wants us to be free of fear so we can be truly free.

We can have attachments to family, friends, partners, jobs, pets, identity of how we see ourselves or how others see us, material things or our belongings. We can become attached to almost anything. It's the result of believing you are not enough without that thing.

Loving and attachment are as different as fear and love. I love my children but do not define myself by them. However, I used to. As I have worked on being unattached, the relationships change. Freeing myself from harsh judgements I had of myself, was necessary to let go. Forgiving myself and accepting the journey I took to get to where I am. Loving them without expectations and attachment brings freedom and expansion. Where attachments bring fear, conditions on love, restriction and at times even pain.

We cannot surrender to our life's path when we are attached to things being as they have been in the past. Attachment inhibits our ability to trust and go with the flow, it's a form of gripping on. What we neglect to see are the objects of our attachment- they are transient and unpredictable, and this is why we feel anxiety and fearful when we have attachments. Attachment is a fear of change, a gripping on, and the need it is attempting to fulfill is a need for safety and security. The remedy to this restrictive behaviour is to let go of trying to find security outside of ourselves. Letting go of control that we have become accustomed to using, as a false sense of safety. We have told ourselves, "If I am in control, everything will be ok". Look around the planet for a moment, how is that working?

I was not in control of my new path opening up in Noosa. I was responsible for it and the choices I made but the more I let go and surrendered, the more magic appeared. What letting go of attachments are not: Letting go can be mistaken for not caring. This is false. It takes great care and focus to detach. Letting go of attachments does not have to mean leaving our loved ones, selling that car, leaving a job or moving away from anything you are attached to, but it may. Letting go is releasing the need we have for the thing or person and the false sense of security it offers. Sometimes for example, in this process we do leave relationships, but this is related to the ending of soul contracts and shifting timelines to match our new frequency.

It can still be done while staying in that job or being a hands-on parent, it's just that us first wavers cut the path as we did and do for many things. We did it tough so that those following would hopefully have a path to follow. Letting go of an attachment is letting go of the false self, when we think this thing or image is who we are. How that story unfolds is a unique journey for each of us.

In order to find out who you are, you need to allow the false self to drop away. For those who haven't yet taken this step; in times ahead and in my understanding, there will be 3 days of darkness when we experience the huge solar flash that I will speak about in more detail in coming chapters. This will be an opportunity to allow this process to occur. When we lose power/lighting, heating, internet, phone connections and other outside distractions, we have no place to go but inside. This is the design and meaning for this event. Sitting with yourself, in what could seem like the nothingness, which is actually your soul, is where you will find everything. It's a process of shifting perspective from the little me (this small identity behind the veil) to the big me (the larger part of myself). This is done by letting go of who you thought you were.

I see this as our greatest attachment, this identity to the ego-self. It can sound a little scary to let go of who we thought we were but as soon as we let go, a feeling of calm will prevail. It's a bit like jumping off a cliff with a parachute, the challenge is taking the leap. Once you've taken the step, the process unfolds. We are letting go of all the fear, karma and struggle, we are separating from the old reality, the old paradigm, from the experience of separation.

It's like a new you is being birthed, where you are moving into a new timeline. It's still you but you will be expressed in a new way. Then the flash of light will have the space to fill you with the expansion of who you really are, and you will feel the greatest peace you could ever imagine.

As for all things, we have a choice with regards to this, to either step forward and choose to let go, or our life presents it to us, seemingly without a choice. It seems to me the timing is tied in with our life plan that we set out before we incarnated. We choose it or it happens for us in divine timing.

Some people experience life changing events such as a stroke or losing their job. These crossroads can be Karmic but often because their grip was so tight on keeping things the same. It's a bit like a prop for this false sense of self who has to feel they are right. The universe stepped in to assist them to see that these things they were attached to, are not in fact, who they are. That the truth is, they are so much more, and their life is trying to show them if they will just surrender to it. Letting go of control of our own lives, or our place in another's, is also a part of what I am referring to as non-attachment.

This is about balance, trust, independence and interdependence, and as you may have already surmised, is fuelled by love.

When happiness and peace of mind are reliant on something or someone outside of us, it affects our emotional stability and clouds our judgement. Then we are directed to make decisions based on fear of loss rather than what's best for us and others. By letting go of the need to define ourselves by these things we are attached to, we uncover and discover who we really are.

I don't think this can be said too often: planet earth is a realm of free-will and therefore there is no right or wrong way to awaken or not to, just your own way and time. Why would we be given free will then be judged for using it?

Let's go back to the title of this chapter, "Shifting dimensions; Embodying soul" and talk about how we are being supported to do this: One of our support systems is the universe, and through this we are given information through the ancient wisdom of astrology. Our wise ancestors referred to the heavens for guidance. Much of this can be researched. There are also a number of documentaries on this subject such as "Ancient apocalypse". Astrology is a tool we have been given to help guide us on this journey and was an ancient science before spirituality and science split and went separate ways. Another example of separation and how that is an illusion. Science and spirituality are like the chicken and the egg, one cannot exist without the other.

One of astrology's definitions is this; a study of movements and relative positions of celestial bodies interpreted as having an influence on human affairs and the natural world.

Much of humanity has seen this ancient realm of science as something to reject or fear. It is said to be referred to in the bible by this quote: (Matthew 23:24, Corinthians 8:6 Exodus 20:3.) "Chasing after false Gods is a sin". It's all in the interpretation. There is reportedly missing text from the bible, they have been reported to have "fallen out of use" or have "not been written by an apostle". So, we can see some gaps, as there are in the meaning given to the text. This is highlighted by the "Missing years of Jesus" written by Dennis Price. Humanity has been known to present information with an agenda rather than as it was intended. Many religions have stated that there is no reference in the bible that says, "God has given authority to the stars or astrologists". When a human is moved to go in a certain direction that is within natural law, it is their birthright to explore that path and discover what it has for them without any exterior authority questioning it. That statement would represent a belief in a God that is outside and separate from us, which was, and to some degree still is encouraged because that disempowers human kind. We are a part of this creator God/Source energy and do not need to be dictated by it as an outside authority. You can do you own research as I always encourage, and see if the bible as we know it, is the full story.

This time is unique in many ways, the placements of the planets and their effect on humanity are some of nature's confirmation and examples of support. We just need to go back through history and look at the current line-up of the planets and the continuation of planetery movement. Then perhaps we can see the effects on mankind when they were in these or similar configurations, earlier in human history.

Astrology shows the history of mankind and offers us an opportunity to learn from the past and make new choices. Everything is connected and supportive of the whole truth.

Now, what I am about to discuss may be a stretch for some readers, but it's impossible to write a book about our evolution and advancement without including the universe and other civilizations. At the same time, it seems a touch arrogant to think this entire universe, or universes exist entirely and exclusively for human beings.

I remember a line from a movie about extra-terrestrials called "Contact", starring Jodie Foster. The scene I'm referring to is where Jody's character talks about the common belief many of us hold: that us humans are the only species in this entire universe but her slant was- if that's the case then what a waste of space. I think I'll leave that there because we are all exactly where we are in our acceptance of other life forms, other galaxies and where ever that is, is ok. Stay tuned as it feels we will have more concrete evidence of spaceship and extra-terrestrials in the coming years. My intention here is that this prepares you a little for the next paragraph.

We have been, and are currently being, supported intergalactically in this journey of ascension and it often goes on either hidden from the mainstream or unacknowledged. Again, please do your own research, there is a lot of information about what has been held back from mainstream news. I find this to be another example of a deeper level of waking up. This support involves star councils, galactic federations and many other beings from other star systems, working together to help our planet and her people continue to bring this shift into reality.

Many of us have star families that are helping. And whether we are conscious of this or not, they are supporting us. This has been going on for many, many years in readiness for this shift which affects the entire universe. This shift not only makes a huge difference here on our planet but in the oneness, we affect everything, everywhere. What we do here on earth ripples throughout the cosmos. That's a responsibility that motivates me to keep going, even when things are difficult.

This is an amazing responsibility that we all share, whether we are aware of it or not. This awareness and natural focus on our oneness and the behaviours that result is the fifth dimensional reality being grounded. It's an everyday awareness where we feel our oneness and know that our every action has a consequence. Whether this behaviour is witnessed by another or not, you know within. As above, so below. What you give out comes back to you. It always has and it always will. As you experience more and more 5D moments, the shift that you encounter is that without any effort loving actions become our response to life.

INCONVENIENT CONSCIOUSNESS

Our innate nature comes from our heart and leads us naturally to always act in everyone's best interest, "for the highest good of all". I am you and you are me, I am you and you are me, I am you and you are me. Do you feel that? When we begin to take this on board and go to an even deeper level where you really know this; the natural consequence is choosing love over fear every time, without exception.

It can be comforting to know there are many levels of support for us at this time. Another support we are receiving energetically is through an increase of light flooding the planet. Light is information and the source of all things. It is the absence of darkness and helps us to see and understand more clearly the true nature of things. Light has a history on our planet although not often discussed, other than in spiritual circles. Exposure to light has been known to heal and rejuvenate body, mind and spirit and to increase well-being. In many religious texts the light symbolizes inner peace, purity and divine presence, guiding us spiritually. It guided me in my experience of the group I joined many years ago and continues to each day.

Shifting to a crystalline body means we can hold more light. I've noticed amongst other things my diet is changing, and I consciously connect to and draw on light and nature to energise me, whereas once I would have looked to food, to do that.

In my meditations recently, I find connecting to the light is getting clearer and easier. Everything is energy and light is energetic information from Source, The Divine/God, The Universe. This light being directed to earth is increasing as our human bodies upgrade to hold more light, which allows us to become more of who we are. It is a tool that helps us transcend this fear-based reality.

This light alters our bodies to be able to ascend into the golden age of our New World of love, the Fifth Dimension. While this ascension process continues, it is easy to be distracted by all the personal dramas, wars, government behaviour, injustice, social media information, standing for this and against that. All of this kerfuffle is what it takes for some people to wake up and can become a big distraction if we allow ourselves to be drawn in. If you are drawn in, it could be helpful to ask yourself what are you wanting to be distracted from? Only you can do your work. The only focus that deserves your attention is the shift that moves your perception from victim to taking responsibility for who you are being in every moment and as a race who we are all becoming.

Only you and your connection to the Divine, God, a higher power, can do this. No guru, no book, no therapist, no retreat or even a unique lifestyle can make you intend this for yourself. Essentially, it's up to you to lift you up, to guide you to the highest version of yourself and to be who you are innately designed to be on this planet.

We were not designed to function in a state of fear, stress, anxiety, separation, lack, disease, pain, forcing and struggle. No surprises there! No one outside of you can make this shift for you. You can choose to enrol a mentor to walk with you, even hold your hand and guide you but this is your work. You can choose to hand the "how" over to a higher power and just focus on "what" you want and use the power of intention to begin.

As you let go of control, needing to know, of doing, of anything weighing you down, no longer taking responsibility for those people and contracts that are now complete. You, choosing you, is imperative. This is for you and everyone else because choosing you means you don't need anyone else to be ok and you show up whole, happy, healthy and abundant. Not needing anyone to match your core wounds so you feel comfortable.

The deepest core wound humans have is abandoning themselves so come back to yourself by choosing yourself. Then you will feel your alignment. Just breathe and follow your bliss, that's it. From there you receive the downloads, hear the wisdom, see the synchronicities, resonating and connecting to those souls who are also self-responsible and on a Sovereign soul journey. Be here now and create, whatever it is you are called to create.

You are ready to see your light and let others see your light. We then see other people's light, then more and more light is ignited. Choose love, really choose love, for you and for everyone else. Yet it starts with choosing you, loving you for the highest good of all. Then share your magic, through whatever excites and ignites you. That's how you will receive miracles beyond your wildest dreams which is what you are designed to do and be. If you feel like you are not getting what you wanted to get by choosing you, it means you deserve better. Just let go and have fun, be free, live limitlessly. It doesn't matter what you're doing, it matters what you're being.

This is embodying your soul …

CHAPTER 6 QUESTIONS:

A) What question if any do you have about something that would help you take your next step, in shifting into 5D?

B) Have you or anyone close to you ever been presented with an opportunity to go into the unknown empty handed? What happened?

C) Do you recognise any area of your life where you have attachments? How are they restricting your life? How can you change this?

D) How valuable is it to you to know more about who you really are and what you are capable of? What will knowing that add to your life?

E) What is your understanding of soul?

F) Would you like to have a more conscious connection with your soul? How would this change your life?

G) Is there anything that would make this ascension process more likely for you to choose and achieve? If so, how will you create that?

CHAPTER 7

MANIFESTATION AND HOW IT WORKS.

For eons and eons, we have been told we must pay to live on this planet and therefore work for the money that this existence costs. You are conditioned to force yourself even if you don't enjoy what you are doing, behaving as a slave because this is just how it is. We have been told that we are different and separate from each other and separate from nature who lives freely and innately supported. Where humanity's belief in separation, our misalignment has even put nature at risk. Such is the unity of all things. What we do to anyone, including nature, we do to ourselves.

This fear-based story of disempowerment took hold, and it may have been further supported by science and spirituality splitting, when they went to war with one another. This reality really took hold in the last third of the nineteenth century, after the publication of Darwin's book on evolution. When we separate anything from the whole of life, it negates the connection and value of the interconnectedness of all things. When we believe in accidents or coincidences which can only be considered when we negate that all things are connected, life loses its magic and purpose and then it becomes haphazard and scary.

Then we believe we are alone and without support. This is a living example of how the lack of unity consciousness causes pain and suffering on our planet. And so began the journey of enslavement, limitation and reliance on exterior means.

From an infant we are taught that life is a hardship and with "Darwin's Theory" tells us we are not connected or supported by anything or anyone. The Divine or any higher power is out of this picture, as we are alone. Every challenge is a fault and needs to be fixed in some way by something or someone outside of us. We are taught that the most valued activity of a human is getting more stuff, and to physically be more comfortable as well as thinking about how to look like we are more.

All the time looking after the ego self, regardless of the cost to others, ourselves or the planet which is our home. It sounds like a recipe for disaster and as it's turned out, it is. Just look at the state of our world. Let yourself feel the grief of that, for just a moment.

When we travel back in history, we find lost civilizations such as Egyptian, Atlantian, Lemurian along with unexplained structures such as pyramids, underground cities, tablets, star directional dials and many such things that are currently being uncovered all around the world. Much of this can be seen on the Netflix documentary, "Ancient Apocalypse" that contradicts the common knowledge of our history, while presenting some challenging new perspectives. These discoveries, although not commonly talked about as yet, beg us to question the limited stories of our past and that includes our capabilities as a human species. It begs us to ask the question, why is this coming to light now?

You may have heard this referred to as everything happens for a reason. And when enough of us shift our frequency, things begin to shift. These beliefs become more real when you give life meaning. This is not a random universe but rather, everything has meaning.

It seems to me these discoveries that are coming to our attention highlight this time on earth as being one of great significance. There is more to the human being than we have been told and how else will we uncover this unless we look in new places? How else will we become more of who we really are unless we explore more of ourselves and make change?

This leads me to the theme of this chapter: "Manifestation". If we humans are capable of so much more, what are we actually capable of? How would things be different if we are capable of manifesting our needs through our innate connection and power of the Divine within? Perhaps it would look like something similar but a little different to nature.

Let's explore a little background of the humans who were hunters and gatherers and, after thousands of years, have ended up here, working for the man. Spending more time at work than with those you love.

We've been conditioned to believe that the only worthwhile information we can source comes from our minds and our learning institutions, are truly filled with repetition of what we already know. As a species we're told this is the way forward, the way to get ahead.

Ahead of what, you might ask? We are ensured that we need authorities watching over us in order to know how to act, what to think, who and what to judge and to tell us what's important, even how to be healthy and happy because, somehow, we are faulty. The thing is, this way of living hasn't worked for our ancestors and so why would it work for us? Isn't that the benefit of history; to see what we could improve on rather than keep doing the same thing regardless?

This conditioning of disempowerment extends to us lacking trust in all levels of ourselves. Telling us we cannot trust our own feelings and that we don't know what's in our best interest. This has fed fear and opened the way for less benevolent beings to take control. Hiding the truth that our bodies can heal themselves and our minds have extraordinary wisdom and are connected to universal intelligence. Even that our words are actually spells, that's why they call it spelling. That we are born equal and sovereign and that one day, very soon I hope, we will wake up to this.

As a Clinical Hypnotherapist, words are all I have to help my clients make their own changes, and these changes improve their lives on a daily basis. This is some of the power that has been hidden from us until now, carefully controlled and enforced. Anyone who spoke up in early history would be made an example of; often tortured and burnt at the stake. Many lightworkers know this journey and some of us have fears of stepping forward into our full power due to these unresolved memories. Personally, I've done a great deal of work to get to this place of sharing the truth. We hold our own ability to let go of the past, to shift, to evolve and empower ourselves to share our wisdom. And it's our birth right not only to share this but to know it and to use it in our own lives.

The drug fuelled medical model want us to believe that our bodies are a meat suit and must fit into this restricted and very sad story. That's how they make over a trillion dollars a year in their focus on illness rather than health. This is done largely by suppression of the body's symptoms, which are messages letting you know what needs attention.

The story goes, we must go to work most of our lives and pay for living on this planet so that someone else gets the financial benefits. If we really stop, take the time to look at what we have signed up for, would we keep putting our energy into it? Sounds exhausting, even a touch insane, right? Yet we often wonder why we are so tired. Tired of this lie and tired of not being true to ourselves by pretending this life is what we want.

My suspicion is that most of humanity including you, suspects that something is just not right, that there must be more. There is nothing wrong with wanting more. Not more stuff but more freedom, more joy, more connection and love, more passion for life, more wellbeing.

I don't know about you, but I don't know many truly happy, healthy, empowered or abundant people who live in this reality. Especially those at the so called "top" because the ego is never satisfied and always wants more. I'm sure you've noticed if you've had a chance to travel, how third world countries seem to have happier, more patient, kind and compassionate people than the wealthier countries. Money is not the problem or the lack of it and we all have the right to abundance, it's how people become attached to it and disconnected through it that causes them pain.

The flip side of this is a motivation for change only really occurs when things get uncomfortable. The question is, are things uncomfortable enough for enough of us yet? If not, then we may be in for some rough times ahead. I say this not to evoke fear but to offer an opportunity for preparation and focus. Everything happens for a reason supports the mantra I use, "Everything happens for me, through me but not to me". "Forewarned is forearmed" as the saying goes, but the reality needs to be acknowledged first. The events ahead of us will serve humanity and those who need to awaken.

It may be time to talk about the good news or the biological facts of what a human being is made up of. Well, a small snippet of who you are to bring some hope and encouragement to you. The human brain has about

100 billion neurons and there are 100 trillion cells in the body. Even without considering anything else, and there is a lot else ... that sounds like a lot of potential to me. Let's talk about what the human being really is and what we are innately capable of: expect your mind to be stretched here if you have not done a lot of questioning of our collective conditioning or haven't done much self-discovery work. If you are still with me reading this, it would appear it's your destiny to be reminded and to consciously know more.

The key here, is to check how you feel inside about what you read. Our feelings don't lie. They cannot be made up, faked or forced.

We can suppress them, ignore them or even judge them but they are what they are: feelings are communication from our soul or higher-self/our wise self. I say this more than once in these pages because repetition is the mother of genius. Feelings are designed to keep us connected to universal intelligence and on the highest time line of our lives. They are our strength and give us a foundation and direction. They are designed to be our own **inner** guidance system. So, do you really need exterior authorities when we have our own built in? If you believe you do, then it's your belief that will attract proof to confirm that for you.

So, let's say we *are* this separate, limited being who needs to be led, directed, kept under control and, of course, live as a slave, because we need to pay our way for just being on this planet!

Why then, if this is a healthy perspective of life and the answer to us being happy is there so much suicide, so many adults and children with mental and physical illnesses, chronic levels of addiction, family violence and breakdowns, wars, racism, classism, sexism and belief-separation, not to forget about life defining poverty. The future of our planet, our precious babies and children, who on our watch on this planet, are being abused, abandoned and dying of hunger. Do you still want to remain asleep?

Why are there so many lonely people? So many people living on the streets without their basic needs being met? Why are so many human beings needing more government support than any time in history? Why is the system set up for disadvantaged people to stay on the system rather than get well? Our living costs are rising at an unreasonable rate, making it more and more difficult for people to find peace about the state of their lives. Could it be because it's time for change?

Let's just explore an alternative perspective that no one who makes money from our limited perspective ever talks about. We are creator sparks. That means we are an aspect of that which creates worlds. Wow, think about that for a few moments... We are aspects or sons and daughters of the Divine... How different is that from what we have been told about ourselves and why is this "news" to so many of you?

Many of us have this as a reality in our lives already but for those who don't, how would that change your life if you really took on this belief? If you were the son or daughter of tall parents with dark skin, would it make sense that you were tall and had dark skin? We are talking about a similar message to what Jesus and the other masters (not gender specific) have tried to share with us. "He (she, they, them) who believes will do the works that I do and greater works than these will he do."

Even though curiosity is a wonderful trait, the reason for our collective ignorance is really not the focus here and if we let ourselves, we could get distracted by that. The key is that we have freewill to believe anything we want and those beliefs, as we have discussed, run our lives. What belief will support you in living your best life? And even if there is resistance to doing this, then great, you've uncovered a gem.

It's helpful to remember what we believe changes our perception and definitely lowers or lifts our vibration and the vibration of the planet. Even when we make personal shifts, it still doesn't change everyone in the collective. Yet the good news is we are no longer at the effect of it or affected by it and when enough of us make the shift it will create the new reality. An example of that is the one hundred metre sprinter, that broke the ten second barrier in the late 1990's. It was unheard of before then and has since been beaten. Even though this is more common now, each one of those sprinters did the necessary work to reach that goal. We are all connected and even able to affect the collective, but each person is required to do their own work.

A belief is simply a thought that we've had, over and over again. Beliefs are another aspect of our free will and come from our mind. They are in the subconscious mind so are not always easy to access. If we want to find out if our belief is a limited one, check if it's a belief that works for your life. For example, if you believe: that "I'm not a good person so don't deserve to be happy," or "people my age carry weight," then they will restrict your life. We can choose to believe that we don't need to make a change in order for things to change but that is denial and doesn't change natural law. A truth or natural law is the way of things, even if the majority of humanity doesn't believe it.

As an adult, with our mind fully developed, what we believe depends on our consciousness level. When a belief is related to natural law, it comes from love. Whatever we believe is our choice. A limited belief is something we have decided from the meaning we have given a life event, from our perceptions. Beliefs can change if we want them to, but natural law will not change. For example, what you do to another, you do to yourself, whether you believe this or not. In order to experience change, something must change.

To know thyself, is a well-known quote and the key to consciousness. There are many paths to know the truth of who you really are. "Paths are many, truth is one". We can only know one another to the degree that we know ourselves, and only see in another that which we have recognised in ourselves. This is quite profound and gives us a deeper meaning to the practice of judging another. It begs the question, who are we really judging? If I lack compassion in myself then that is what I see in another. When I am compassionate, I see life through this filter, even if another is not consciously coming from this place. I see the compassion behind the behaviour.

Our perception colours our world. For example: when a person establishes a foundation to help dogs in Bali; those who have closed their heart and projecting self-judgement may see that as a platform for recognition whereas those who are coming from an open heart and compassion will see the love driving this person.

Judgement is another tool of separation and is born of ignorance and a belief that there is only one way- "my way". Yet mostly this is a practice of projecting the disowned self. I see the part of myself that I have disowned or judged as being faulty in you, and I do this for the reason of learning to love all parts of myself. Judgement is about right and wrong, lacking acceptance of the individual's expression. When a person puts being right above everything else, they will suffer. If I must be right about my view of this person, then it inhibits me from seeing anything else. We can choose to be right or to be happy, to be right or to experience peace.

For most of our memory on this planet there has been an existence of polarity- right and wrong, good and bad, black and white etc and this has served us to learn how opposite things can co-exist. However, this way of living creates separation and pain. Dare we stop comparing and just be in the moment of how life is unfolding? Not right or wrong, not good or bad, just life unfolding with the opportunity to perceive it any way we choose.

Manifestation is the name given to the power of how we bring things into our experience, how we create creation. We have been taught that we need to have money to do things and the fact that we all have differing amounts of the stuff, shows the inequality in this major energy exchange. Most people sell their time for the stuff and even base their self-worth on the numbers in their bank account. This condition creates limitation and a condition on our freedom. In a way, it could be seen as a form of control and another tool of separation.

What if living abundantly and in freedom was not reliant on the amount of work you do or time you spend at work but something much more accessible to all of us? In fact, your wealth has nothing to do with selling your time, money or the amount of it we have or don't have.

It has everything to do with the power of our thoughts and beliefs especially those about our worthiness. We manifest by using the power of our thoughts, imagination, visualisation and feelings because we are creator sparks, and this happens even if we are unconscious of the process.

There are some exclusions to this formula such as people who are destined through their life's path to have abundant finances to support their journey or mission. There are also people who are learning life lessons from having an abundance of money. There is no such process that is happening always, for everyone. In other words, some people's life path is set and it requires abundance in the form of money and material things to complete it. For example, such people as Richard Branson who has, what might be seen as an empire with over two hundred companies which flows onto employing a minimum of seventy thousand people, serving approximately 53 million customers. He started his first charity, "Student Valley Centre" when he was seventeen years old and today supports thirty-seven other charities. Some of these are: African Wildlife Foundation, Free the Children, Girls Not Brides, Save the Elephants, Water.Org, Peace One Day, Whatever it Takes, and more. A charity is ideally defined as an organisation whose entire purpose is to assist the community without a focus on self-gain. These souls would appear to have chosen a life path that could not be fulfilled without attracting billions of dollars.

You might be asking now, why don't we know how we manifest our lives already? I think I've addressed some of the reasons, but this is also due to the timing of our evolution. We have, in past civilizations, through negative influences and the level of consciousness of the collective at the time, misused our innate abilities and created a nightmare, and, in many ways, we still are.

Just before the fall of Atlantis for example, we began to experiment with animals and human body parts and later with dark matter, trying to create worm holes that collapse our grids. These activities go against natural law and had to be stopped by the keepers of the earth grid.

There are scientific experiments going on today that are heading down this same track, animal parts being transplanted into humans and attempts to create worm holes, without reverence for the effects of these experiments. Man's law has overtaken nature's law but in truth nature will always prevail. This is an example of where science has separated from spirituality and the threat of harm this can cause. This happens when we focus on the small self or ego-self and its wants which are primarily power and control. We must first evolve into unity consciousness to know what we create affects all of us, so we can create for the highest good of all.

This great wake-up call or Ascension into a higher level of consciousness is a process that strips away fear and separation. It clarifies nature's law from man-made law, and we return to trusting in our inner guidance or higher-self who is our divine connection to Source.

As we allow the false self to drop away, the part of us that thought we were separate and limited, then more of who we are, comes to the surface and is grounded in our lives. Ignorance and confusion are fear, knowledge and clarity are love. In this process we become that which we truly are. Then love is the new currency, the new motivation and all there ever really is.

This is why it takes as long as it takes, and why only you can do it for yourself. Patience for ourselves and each other is called for because we must be thorough. The false self has lived in separation and is motivated by fear and our true self lives in unity and harmony and is motivated by love. Unlike our past experiences, this is a different time as we let go and ascend, we will manifest for the highest good of all as a natural course of events. It becomes our new perspective because we have returned to who we are.

As you look around our planet do you see any examples of this? I can think of one that is in question and that's Woodside Fuel. The First Nations people have already put a hold on gas exploration as well as one of the devices they want to use; a sound radar that would damage breading of our marine life, which is our future. Many levels of nature would also be violated. Greenpeace are taking them to court to challenge how honestly

Woodside Fuel represent their activities. It's worth keeping in mind most of these big companies are attempting to cover their tracks because they are profit focused.

So, in many cases they have yet to be held accountable as is for many structures of society that are being exposed as redundant. I hope these profit fuelled companies will, in time, be held accountable as our values reflect our connection to nature. I would like to acknowledge and thank the brave warriors who are on the frontline of these exposures, highlighting the need for change in environmental areas.

The time is fast approaching for those of us doing work on ourselves by releasing fear, to begin expanding our innate abilities. This will happen organically through our shift in energy and what is known as "The law of attraction". The empowerment we feel as a result will draw us together to create communities where we will focus on our soul's mission, because we are stronger together.

A part of this new earth is to know and use the power that we are and to consciously manifest our hearts desires. Lack is fear based, everything you need is available before you even know you need it. All hearts have wonderfully unique desires for a better world, but we also have one in common- this is "peace on earth and peace for all mankind". We know this formula and without any road map, step by step, this is how we create "Heaven on Earth", or our "New World".

Recently, in our known history, many of mankind's creations have been unconscious. That is, they have been created from the unconscious mind, based on past unresolved wounds. These are events from the past that we didn't think we could deal with, so we suppressed them. These actions have often been out of our conscious awareness, that's how the unconscious mind functions. It takes awareness and intention to make conscious, our unconscious beliefs and behaviours. For example, segregation of black and white people that was made law several times in the nineteenth and twentieth century in America. It was believed to be the result of a general opinion around different coloured people being unable to coexist.

As humanities awareness raised and we became more conscious of the pain caused by this separation, civil rights activists such as Clarence Mitchell Jr., Rosa Parks and Martin Luther King Jr helped to eventually bring about a somewhat more conscious way to live.

The environmental damage in all its forms has been the result of unconscious thoughts and actions. They are old patterns that are no longer working. From the plastic found in our water ways that kill and maim our marine life to the deforestation that is still occurring at an alarming rate all around the globe. Between 2010 and 2020, the net loss in forests globally was 4.7 million hectares (H Ritchie). Coral reefs only cover a small percentage of the vast ocean, but they're home to about twenty-five percent of all ocean species. Unconscious actions have led to pollution, over fishing and physical destruction of our reefs. These are just some of our unconscious fears and beliefs that have, and still are, creating havoc. As we do our personal work to heal from the past, bringing what was in our unconscious into our conscious awareness this releases fear and as a result returns us to the knowledge of our connection to everything.

A new consciousness and choice are being birthed: to firstly know who we are and then to ground this in our lives by consciously manifesting or creating for the highest good of all. And, of course, for the joy of it. War is an example of this. We consciously know it doesn't produce the positive change or intent held by those in charge, but it is still going on. My understanding of this behaviour is fuelled by the ancient war and separation thought forms endowed upon us eons ago. As we keep owning these thought forms, we will see war become a thing of the past.

The new reality where we ground through actioning our oneness, allows us to know of our unity and really feel it. When we feel something, it can't be denied, it moves from our head to our heart and then it becomes a part of us. Once we know this, we can't unknow it. A bit like the corn kernel popped, it will never go back to being a kernel, and this is how shifts occur. Manifestation's intention returns to a focus on unity, innately loving and simply for the joy of it.

Finally, we are ready to talk about the formula. Do not fear, this cannot be brought into existence until the person using it is ready or has done the work to be a clear channel. It simply won't work. This is the perfection of the universe and is one of the natural laws of cause and effect.

Our thoughts, feelings and other senses (such as visualisation, imagination and an intent mindset) can be used to manifest. The clearer and more specific the information we focus on, the clearer and more spot on the manifestation will be. Focus is consciousness and consciousness is love, therefore your clarity of focus is the creative energy of creation. What we focus on magnifies.

In truth, we have been manifesting our reality since the beginning of time, but the key now is the change that changes everything. We can do it consciously from the energy of love and without attachment. You will hopefully remember; attachment is about thinking you **must** have something outside of yourself in order to be whole or ok. It is a gripping on, holding tight energy and it's based in fear. We are whole already and when we know this by letting go of all that is not us, we manifest for the joy of it and abundance flows freely.

I'll give you an example of an attached desire and old patterns forming the foundation of a desire to manifest: Let's say I want to manifest a new car. I decide which car I want, the colour and all the inclusions. I go ahead and use the power of my imagination to see myself in this beautiful new car. I can even smell that new car smell as I imagine sitting behind the wheel. I think about having the car and how that feels to have it parked in my garage, how people will see me as successful because I own this flash car. I tell myself; I really need this because then I'll be happy. I think about this obsessively, around fifty times a day but still it doesn't appear.

This outcome matches what I really believe. I believe that without this car I am not whole so I don't manifest it. Which only confirms my deepest fears of unworthiness and limitation. This lack of manifestation is telling me that the energy behind my desire is fear of not being enough without this car. I definitely have an attachment, but it also shows old limited patterns and beliefs. Deep down I feel less than, I have limited beliefs about my worthiness. Currently, I drive an old car which I judge as failure and want to be seen as successful so I'm attached to having this new car. I think it will make me feel better on the inside by changing the outside. However, it doesn't materialise.

Versus, I want to manifest a new car because that would be so much fun, I am worthy of having a car that feels beautiful to drive. I have done work on myself worth and like who I am and my life as it is. I use my imagination to see myself in this car, the make, the model and the colour I want. I see myself driving with my loved ones and feel the joy of that. I even have a test drive of this new car. I smell that new car smell and hear the beautiful sound system, the quietness of the motor and smoothness on the road. I even put a photo of this car up on my fridge and fall in love with how it looks but don't brag about getting it. Instead, I think about the fun I will have when it arrives. I check in with myself to ensure I am unattached to how and when this will manifest and then I get on with my life, knowing it will arrive at the perfect time for everyone. My new car arrives, the manifestation is complete.

Another example of this process is the desire to have a conscious and loving partner. Not to complete me as I have worked diligently to know my wholeness. Not to make me happy as I take responsibility for that, not to fill some void as only I can do that for myself but for the absolute joy, love and expansion this union will bring into my life and the lives of those around us. I get very specific about this partner's qualities, so the universe knows what I want. There is no right or wrong desire when it brings us, and the world, joy, which is really saying, when it is for the highest good of all.

I want to attract a single man who is doing work on himself and is living consciously, he is open hearted, responsible for himself, his life and is financially independent. He is healthy and active, and we have a mutual attraction to each other, body, mind and soul. He has had the courage to release old karmic relationships and enjoys healthy, close connections to those who really know him. He wants to make a difference in the world and is inclusive in his benevolent actions, our missions are compatible. He is supportive in general and in what is important to me, as I am with him. He is generous, compassionate, loving, passionate and connected. He has a healthy level of self-esteem, and we can both give and receive love.

After knowing what I want I go about using my thoughts, imagination and senses. I then day dream and imagine having him in my life, cooking dinner together, going for beach walks, travelling together, spending quality time with our loved ones who value themselves and us, doing things together that we feel aligned to. I feel connected, nurturing and nurtured. We really see each other because we know ourselves. I feel excited about the endless possibilities that our lives offer us. I feel loving and loved, I feel calm and balanced, we both do. I give of myself to him as he does to me with surrender and passion. We are good for each other. I hear his laughter and his kind words of encouragement, his vulnerability and offers to help. I think about the places we might travel to and adventures we embark upon. I hear, see and feel our family and friend's get togethers that we enjoy and the happiness we share. We both feel grateful for this blessing and union that has expanded our lives in joy filled ways. I check in with myself to ensure I am unattached to how and when this will manifest. I then allow the universe to weave it's magic and get on with my day.

Every part of our lives is about intention. The Universe responds to our intention. Ask yourself, "What is my true intention for this manifestation? Is it a fear-based intention which will be about lack, my life or myself not being enough? Perhaps it's a negative belief or program of behaviour. Or does it come from a place of love and joy? Once you have that answer and have made any necessary shifts, then you are ready for the first stage of manifestation. You have the steps, practice, be honest with yourself and have fun.

I want to share a second stage of manifestation, not better or worse than the steps already given. This is for those who are in a more advanced stage of making the shift: through our consciousness we are becoming our mission and the energy of manifestation. With our vibration high, we focus on what is for the highest good of all and it is here. We are not given all the steps on how to do things, we are moving past questioning ourselves and trusting in what is coming through. This process builds trust with us, our guides and each other. Be assured you will receive the support needed. *Keep going, holding the power of who you are and being solid in that. This is the most powerful thing you can do.* If you get angsty or old patterns come up, remember "That sounds like the old me, I don't do that anymore". It's a reassurance for the unconscious mind that in fact, you are safe with this change. Remind yourself this is what you are here to bring. Believe it, receive it, be it. This is what you are here to do.

These are the formulas for conscious manifestation. I use them, many people do, and they are available to everyone no matter their current experience in life. You can do it; you are a creator by nature. It's your birthright. You will be delighted and surprised just how simple it is. So go ahead, test it out and enjoy creating your version of heaven on earth.

CHAPTER 7 QUESTIONS:

A) What percentage of you believes you are capable of manifesting your heart's desires and living the life of your dreams? If you want this to be higher, how will you do this?

B) Can you remember a time when you have manifested something that almost seemed miraculous? How did you do that? What was the flow on effect on your life?

C) Is there an aspect of your fearful/wounded self that believes you are not enough? How has this effected your life? How much better can this be?

D) What do you understand about being non-attached to the outcome, as a necessary step to manifestation? How will knowing that look for you?

E) Is there any step in the process of manifestation that you would like clarity on?

F) If so, how will you resolve this?

G) Knowing you can manifest whatever your heart desires; what would you absolutely love to manifest in your life personally and for the world?

H) Knowing that you are limitless, what is your vision for our world?

CHAPTER 8

LOVE, THE VERY ESSENCE OF CREATION.

The heart is the first organ to develop in utero, even before the brain. Many medical mystics such as Rudolf Steiner and Dr Thomas Cowan have suggested that rather than being a pump, it propels and regulates the blood. They go on to say that the heart is a spiritual development organ, another aspect of potential about the human that is being brought to light. We can with our intention, connect our heart to our brain consciously and so our every thought, word and action comes from love.

We've already spoken about the consciousness shift or Ascension that is in progress, and at its core this is all about transcending fear and returning to love. Yet we need to talk about what the hurdles have been to experiencing love in our collective lives.

This Ascension is both an individual journey and, at the same time it is a collective one. There will continue to be big moments that are designed to move us forward. Along the way we will most likely experience more solar flashes, (which are a huge flash of solar energy from the sun) that will give us a giant leg up, as well as possible tidal waves, earth rifts and other events that are outside of normal experiences. These events have been written about in spiritual circles and many people have had dreams, visions and guidance about them. It's never designed to elicit fear, but rather, tells us what it might take for some people to wake up.

I find when the same information keeps showing up and coming from different resources, it speaks to being forewarned or given preparation time. In such events you are being given an opportunity to walk your talk and hold your light strongly.

The remaining shifts come from us and our own inner work. In particular, the acceptance of who we are, which allows us to make peace with all parts of ourselves. There are aspects of us all, often referred to as our shadow self, parts we'd rather avoid that require our ownership. They have served us on our 3D journey but are no longer relevant.

I've mentioned the power of being in the present moment in your life and while this is the way forward, it can seem confusing when I speak about owning your past shadows while being in the present moment. What I mean by this is most of our wounding happened in the past, but those wounding's are alive within us now even if they have been suppressed or have gone unacknowledged, as our negative feelings and emotions. They can only be accessed here and now and therefore healed here and now. We can't feel a feeling in the past, we can only feel it now. There is no need to relive or become those old experiences and memories, we want to become the spiritual observer. Getting in touch with the feeling of the experience is all we need to do to release it.

These old memories are useful and fleeting, designed to trigger the emotion that needs to be felt, in order to be healed and released. Our intention is to comfort that inner-child, past trauma from the modern-day self that you are now.

As I often say to my clients, "That was then and this is now and things are different, in a good way". Acceptance of ourselves and our experiences is essential. We feel rejected by life when we don't love ourselves. When we feel limitation, suspicion, judgement or hesitation, we are falling backwards to how things used to be. This is an example of a life event trigger.

Any time we are resistant to any part of ourselves, it's like we place a giant rock in the river of our own lives. The rock is in the river of our vibration. It blocks our flow. The more rocks we place there, the more struggle we experience in our lives. The intention is to remove as much friction as we can. This is how we raise our frequency.

Doing this work is making peace with all aspects of who you are by accepting your unique journey. We can move from this to awareness without judgment, seeing where we can step up to be more of who we are. This shift includes moving into the new reality of trust in self. Bringing those old wounds that has made you judge yourself and others into the present moment and healing them by really acknowledging and accepting all parts of yourself. This is your key to freedom.

Remember, your thoughts can create your perceptions, and your perceptions create your reality. We are moving from a Karmic path: where we are creating and learning from the past to a Dharmic path: where we are creating and learning from our life in the present moment.

Then we are no longer creating from limited beliefs from past wounds and trauma, when we were desperately trying to understand ourselves. We are moving into learning from life in the moment from a place of self-love. The focus this shift takes, is returned to you for the rest of your existence.

I had an experience of this learning from life in the moment today, while taking part in a zoom Hypnotherapy supervision group. One of the therapists (we will call Iona), has been practising counselling for over 20 years and had always been booked out, reported that her practice had gone quiet. She shared how she was "Feeling depressed because of this" and although she had "largely increased her marketing recently, nothing had changed".

She had cleared her space of any discordant energy and done muscle testing to be certain she was not meant to retire just yet, as she was in her seventies. These questions were answered as, "not an issue". So, it seemed to her, it was a marketing issue. Perhaps an open question to the universe such as, "Is there another reason that I haven't discovered yet?" may have opened up new insights.

This was an opportunity, as I saw it, to see what was happening underneath the temptation to want something to blame. To look for a gift the universe was offering her. She said, it was the fact that her business wasn't attracting clients that fuelled her depression. In that moment her life was showing her something. She was manifesting a feeling of depression to highlight her resistance. This was a trigger. The story is just the story, not the cause. She was happy when her business was busy and things were as they had been but now, they had changed, and she was struggling.

It can be so easy to miss a trigger and blame the feeling about the story of our life. That's what happened here, even though this lady was a therapist herself. We often benefit from an outsider's perspective; I know I do. We all have scotomas. It seemed to me this was an attachment she had that her higher-self wanted her to identify by taking it away. If by her business being quiet, she was triggered through feelings of depression, she has a wound in this area. On an energetic level, depression is often a suppression of emotion and can be masking a deeper wound. Her life in the present was showing her a fear that was still controlling her but she didn't see it in that moment. That's ok of course, wherever we are is ok. Yet the question I like to ask is- is it working for her?

Everything happens in waves. The wave is not the water, the water told us of the wave moving by. The event that caused the trigger is not the problem, the trigger itself is not the problem, depression is not the problem in this story, it is telling us of a wound that requires attention.

It could be a feeling of unworthiness that comes up if she is not in demand. When we know everything is leading us to our highest good, we begin to look a little deeper than the outside events. She was not asking for therapy to take responsibility for her feelings but rather wanted to know how to get more clients because she thought this was her answer. To me it was just a band aid. This could have been an opportunity for Iona to use her life's path in the present to learn from and create from. Then she could move forward free of these negative emotions, confusion and lack.

I wasn't asked to offer my input, so I didn't give it. I heard her request for what she wanted and respected that. There are many ways to see most things, and this was mine. Not right or wrong, just my observation. We all see life from our own lens but at the same time can allow others their own perception. How each of us saw it was perfect for our individual journey.

When we make this shift, it feels like we are straddling two worlds: being an observer of the 3D world while living from a love-based reality of 5D. From here there is only acceptance of our life's path and those around us, and with that, comes peace.

Love is at the centre of our lives, whether we are aware of it or not. It is not only the essence of who we are but without it we would perish. Love is innate within humans because love is who we are, I think we've always known this. Even in the darkest of experiences and when we've felt abandoned and alone, love has been calling to us. In those moments it's the lack of love that causes us so much pain. It beckons us through the pain of its absence, to remind us of this truth.

At this stage in our evolution love needs to be nurtured. An example of this is a newborn infant's developmental stage of eye gazing. It's vital for both emotional and intellectual wellbeing. It has special significance in early attachment and bonding and plays an important part in the process of gaining information about the world and emotions. When the baby sees the parent's eyes and face, they start making associations between food and feeder, between voices and persons, between a smile and what it means to be happy or loved.

This developmental milestone is significant in helping children develop capacities to be calm and regulated, engage and relate to others. Also, to initiate and respond to different types of communication.

As the baby matures and they are able to follow the caregivers gaze, infants share important information with parents. This is an essential skill to enjoy play and essential to the development of language and vocabulary. Babies who are fed and kept warm but not held, nuzzled and hugged enough can stop growing and if the situation lasts long enough, can even die. Such is the universal design which calls us to our very essence, and such is the power of love.

As we mature into an independent being we become responsible for our experiences including giving, receiving, being loving and being loved. When we get clear on what our own needs are and get better at meeting those needs in a positive way, we support our overall wellbeing. And rather than searching for exterior gratification and temporary fixes, we find our answers come from within us and that process guides us towards personal responsibility and consciousness. Our evolution really is an inside job. As a consequence, our life becomes an experience of deeper fulfilment, health and happiness.

It seems essential to include our inherent programming and how that effects our life and relationships which are a main source of love on earth. Similar to our DNA, we inherit our ancestors unresolved fears, giving our families yet to be born, every chance to be free of the old fear-based paradigm. These wounds are passed on and experienced from both our father and mother-lines. This has gone on for generations as is does in all families, both past, present and would be our future generations if we didn't do the work to release it. That speaks to the inconvenience of doing inner work, both for us and the people in our lives. Regardless of that, this has real value for everyone in our families now and for generations to come.

In my experience when I do a clearing such as this, it shifts not only my energy, experiences and timeline but those of my children and it even flows on to generations to come. This is because what we pass on, has changed. We not only inherit ancestral wounds, but we can also clear these for them. This is evolution of the species.

The process I refer to now is what I know as "Healing the mother wound". You can copy this and even make it your own. It shows the many aspects of this wounding that we carry from past generations and how to release them. This example may give you a deeper understanding why family patterns occur and why we have struggled in ways, that don't even feel like our own. Remembering the power of our word in this process I use the word "clear" and declared from spirit, a clearing of all of this.

This process is fluid and can be adjusted to suit. You will need around fifteen to twenty minutes so you can come back to this if needed or continue now. Find a comfortable position to begin, lying down or sitting somewhere you have space and won't be interrupted. You can begin by asking for energetic protection such as Saint Germaine, the Violet Flame Angels, Archangel Michael, your Higher-Self, your Guides or whomever you prefer. It is your intention to set up energetic protection and support that matters. Then you can call in a cleansing ray of light, golden white to continue flowing all through your energy fields, while this clearing is in process.

I will include the wording after explaining the process. Then I request a clearing of any old discordant programs and patterns, any unprocessed trauma or disturbances experienced by my mother and received by me or passed down to me in the womb. I then request clearing concerning anything limiting or toxic passed down to her from her mother and her mother's mother. Remember there is no blame here, it has just been the way things have been up until now. I then asked spirit to clear any victim mentality received in the womb.

Most women in the past had a very unsupportive role in pregnancy, right through to giving birth and for many into mothering. The female experience has been less than empowering and respectful on this planet, for thousands of years. I ask to clear any feelings of abandonment, neglect, unworthiness, being unloved or unwanted, that has been picked up while being in the womb of my mother.

Say these words: "Spirit release, clear and remove any programming I have received from my mother line relating to abuse, bullying, humiliation, shaming, unhealthy modelling of aggression and power, any parent child enmeshment. Clear all disturbances of all the women in my mother line touching me now, including all of the physical, emotional, mental, verbal and sexual abuse. Spirit, release, clear and remove any programming I have received from the women in my father line, related to all the patriarchal dominance, bullying, degradation, shame, guilt and fear. Clear any physical, emotional, mental, sexual abuse experienced by the women in my father line touching me now. Clear any unhealthy patterns relating to the feminine, any impulse towards self-hatred, self-sacrifice, self-sabotage, self-harm, self-punishment. Clear any attachment or cording with my mother or upgrade those connections to a higher bond of love. Clear and cleanse all of my chakras of any enmeshment with my mother. Clear any blocking mental energies that inhibit the activation of my full potential and destiny. Spirit release, clear, dissolve, remove any overt or subtle messages received from my mother that in anyway interferes with my innate abilities and gifts, modes of expression, confidence, courage, chosen direction, identity and values. Anything that adversely effects my direction and destiny.

Remove any conditioning of being compliant, a super people pleaser, an over giver, or seeking to be invisible or seeking to take the blame or any kind of doormat."

"Clear any programs manifesting in my relationships due to the mother wound, such as a fear of abandonment, fear of rejection, any fear of rocking the boat, speaking my truth, any inability to trust another. Clear any struggle concerning intimacy, anywhere my boundaries have been weak or non-existent, anywhere I have been overpleasing, over giving, over clingy, over independent or aloof. Clear any energies and cording's I have received in any intimate relationship or friendship where I have been working through anything to do with my mother wound. Spirit, assist me in finding forgiveness of myself and my mother withing this wounding. I ask for Angelic and crystal healing that promotes any form of healing and self-love that I'm needing, to be completely free of any ancestral wounding".

"Spirit, assist me in realising the multi-dimensional gifts of the mother wound such as the gift of awareness of the suffering generated by the outgoing patriarchal systems. The gift of freedom to seek new spiritual paths, finding new methods of healing. The gifts of seeking new ways for the masculine and feminine to relate with one another. The gift of appreciating the divine feminine in all of her mystical forms and the gift of responsibility for releasing struggle and embracing our new life".

"I ask for this clearing through all minds, bodies, timelines, incarnations and universes. Completely and one hundred percent removing anything that would seek to recreate any of this. Spirit, clear, seal and heal any wounding, openings, tears to my energy fields with light. Healing and sealing anything created as a result of this clearing and removal. I evoke this clearing for my highest good and greatest joy. I call upon my higher-selves and guides to step into my love-based highest time line from this moment onwards". After completing this process, I suggest you take some quiet time to allow for integration.

Many of the past generations didn't discuss their traumas or pains. They were, through necessity, focused on survival, and therapy wasn't even something they considered. They simply couldn't afford the luxury. People of this era rarely shared any of their struggles or internal experiences with anyone, for all kinds of reasons. Including feelings of being judged, guilty, unloved, shamed, abandoned, alone, unsafe. Many of our parents and grandparents kept their past wounds to themselves. This is why we often don't even know what we have inherited or what we are playing out that doesn't belong to us. This is why living consciously is so vital to our evolution.

I write this now with a careful mind of giving helpful examples while at the same time keeping confidentialities. There was enormous shame attached to many of the past traumas and secrets of our families, it's with the greatest compassion I share some of this.

Some of my families' secrets and traumas were shared with me in my adult life. As past generations aged and felt enough time had passed to be able to speak of such things. I was told that my female line had many of the traumas that far too many families experience; including sexual abuse, which included abandonment of not being protected or believed. Being born "illegitimate" as they referred to children born outside of marriage, back then, being unwanted and feeling shameful.

Being abandoned by their parent who was unable to be there emotionally due to their own trauma. This abandonment is less obvious and could even be seen as a form of gaslighting. It is very confusing and painful because the parent seems to be physically present. The shame and low self-worth that came with these experiences for both the child and the parent still needs to be released by later generations.

Many stories were told of how women were degraded for all kinds of reasons, powered over and controlled by males. These are just a few of the wounding experiences of my ancestors, past on through the mother-line. It would appear to me that this is the case for most families, although the stories will be different. Considering the challenging days of our history, would suggest there were more, many more. In order to create a new world, we must acknowledge, heal and release the past.

These are some of the programs that were passed on to myself and my children. Each of us, through earlier contracts, have our own particular themes to heal. Is it any wonder we've had challenges, right? This is why we see family patterns; they continue until someone is willing to own them and release them.

This is one of the blessings of living consciously, when we self-reflect, we have a chance to connect the dots, to see family patterns. We have to play these patterns out through our behaviours, in order to see them. We need to own them, take responsibility for them, in order to know what needs to be cleared. I know for myself, I have been shocked at times, playing out behaviours that didn't seem like me. As it's turned out, this is our service to humanity. I wonder if you have experienced anything like this in your own life?

The female ancestors in most of our families and in the world at large have been and still are being powered over and controlled or treated unequally. It's not only women but they make up the large majority. There are some men who are also bullied by both men and women, but this too is an example of the out of balance male energy dominating the female energy. Even in first world countries such as Australia, many women are still addressing the inequality of our wages and workplace conditions and opportunities for advancement. This inequality can be more covert, and both are an example of the history of our ancestors playing out in todays unbalanced patriarchal society.

For many of us this patriarchal age is being recognised as a living example of the imbalance of our individual male/female aspects within ourselves. This balancing of our energy is required for the balance of our planet and shift into our new world.

I am determined to have this fear-based heritage end with me. It is underneath much of the pain that the girls in my family, including myself, as well as my friends and clients, have experienced. As I'm sure yours have as well. How can we create a world based in love without cleaning this up? Here is a message for the unconscious mind, that has its own language. It will receive this in the most appropriate way for you: *"we will clean this up, you know. Humanity needs the return of the feminine gifts. Women deserve respect, acknowledgment and equality. Women and men are equal aspects of creation. We bring our female and male aspects together in unity and love. Yes, we do, and we have, that's right, yes, we did."*

There are learnings opportunities that come with any experience, but if we suppress the experience, then the learnings get put on hold. As we face our experiences and release the emotion, this enables us to embody the learning, the gift the experience offers us.

I have found compassion to be the mother of love, and the road through these challenging behaviours, that our ego self wants to take personally. We've all inherited something that can be difficult to be around, while we go through the process of transmuting it. Some of us choose to take responsibility for our life, own and heal it, and others don't. How easy it can be to blame and judge. The truth is we don't have all the information to judge, and blame keeps us stuck. Whereas taking responsibility frees us. You may have heard the saying- "Everyone is doing their best; with the knowledge they have at the time" but I like to add to this- "although some people are not doing what is best by you" which allows us space to value ourselves within this awareness. Boundaries allow us to take our energy back, to grow our own lives.

Allowing abuse is not compassion and it's not empathy. Enabling is not kindness, not to the person projecting or to yourself. Boundaries are a demonstration of self-compassion. Compassion like all things, begin with the self.

I am eternally grateful for this Aquarian age that we are in now, where things that were once hidden are becoming clear. Have you noticed? Things that we missed before, are becoming obvious now. We are being given every opportunity to wake up, open our eyes and see the truth of what is before us. Only things brought out into the open can be addressed.

Abraham Maslow was an American psychologist who created Maslow's hierarchy of need. A theory of psychological health predicated on fulfilling innate human needs in priority, culminating in self-actualization. Perhaps this reflects the evolution of humanity and can be seen as a worthwhile exploration.

The book "The five love languages", by Dr Gary Chapman is an insightful awareness of how each of us has a love language. He talks about the languages being; "words of affirmation," "acts of service," "giving and receiving gifts," "quality time" and "physical touch." These are the languages that we use to show and receive love. I think it's quite amazing that every single human speaks these languages, we just have them in our own order of significance. He says, if the people in our lives don't give us love in the way we relate to, we can struggle to feel loved. I found this book very helpful in understanding more about myself but also for understanding my children's needs for love and those close to me.

One of the most helpful points Gary makes is: that we give love in the same way we need to be shown love, so that can be a tip if you're trying to clarify someone's love language. This book has sold over 20 million copies and has been written in more than fourteen languages, so it would appear we all speak the same group of love languages.

I can't help but wonder if these languages represent the childhood wounds we are seeking to fill. As we evolve our heart opens more fully and perhaps to some degree, these love languages begin to feel less valid. It seems to me as we embody the love that we are more fully, then we also see love in everything and everyone. In this process there are even new channels of the heart that open, and we are naturally drawn to being more loving, which is, after all, our true nature. Having said this, I still feel a deeper connection in relationships through my main love languages- "words of affirmation" and "quality time".

As my pathway continues to open up and unfold, I keep an open mind. I suspect as my inner child is fully healed and no longer seeks what she didn't get when she was growing up, my love language may also become more universal. Time will tell, my journey will show me.

As the illusionary or separate self drops away and who we really are surfaces, it changes us not only on the surface but within our perception which governs our life. In the process of returning to a loving expression, the shadow self is acknowledged, owned and accepted. This allows us to drop judgements of ourselves and others and unites all parts of our inner self. This experience of believing we are separate has manifested into the need to unite all of our individual aspects. Bringing all our parts together- physically, emotionally, mentally and spiritually. This is the wholeness we long for.

Judgements are a way we have kept ourselves separate from each other and our true self. In truth, there is nothing to judge and nothing to fear because all experience serves us. They are neither right or wrong but rather our way of learning and experiencing from this human life. When we understand this and drop the judgement of ourselves, we also drop judgement towards our fellow travellers because that disowned self that used to annoy us, no longer does.

As we uncover our essence and embrace all of our self and our experiences, we return to being love. In this moment everything changes, it feels as if by a miracle we suddenly feel love for everyone and everything. This often brings me to tears, I have found the feeling of connection that I've longed for, within me. When your joy levels raise, you will feel happy more of the time without an exterior reason. It feels like bliss. At other times it's a feeling of contentment where everything seems different in a good way.

The colours are brighter, the world looks more beautiful, we get green lights more often, synchronicities increase, and we see the good in everything. This is a state we can actually achieve naturally. I know this from experience, and I call it a blissful state of awareness. This is the New Earth, 5D reality where we live in a state of unity, love, joy, abundance and wellbeing. There will still be growth in this reality as that is the nature of the universe, but it will be through the Dharmic path.

Most of us have heard of and maybe even enrolled a Guru on this path of self-discovery. Let's talk about the word guru for a moment, it means an influential teacher or guide and in Sanskrit the Gu stands for darkness and Ru stands for light. So, we could say a Guru is an influential teacher or guide who brings what is in the darkness into the light.

Why should I be introducing such a word? The essence of this book is shining a light that illuminates your unique path to embrace the truth and magic of your mission. All without having to sacrifice your values and your soul. In fact, it's truly my heart's mission as it is for many of us here at this time, to support (the lightworkers, Blue Rays,

Star-Seeds, Indigos) all of us with our sacred mission as we help and serve as pioneers with this paradigm shift.

This journey of reclaiming self-worth is, at its roots, about breaking free from feelings of unworthiness. When you rediscover and reawaken your value and gain confidence to embrace your sacred mission with clarity, you will ignite the remembrance of that passion. This is when true evolution begins to take place. What used to feel difficult, feels easier. It feels more open and allowing, while giving clarity of direction.

There has been a lot of new age spiritual deception, and it's created confusion to some degree. This deception is about believing that the world will change just by spiritually by-passing it: praying for it to change, thinking enough positive thoughts, meditating on world peace. If this was the case, then it would have already happened. As well there is this message that being spiritual means we don't need money. And then there's the idea called, "Let's pretend we are already in 5D". The truth about this last note is that fifth dimensional and higher consciousness is pouring in, but we are not living in 5D consciousness just yet. Take a look around the planet.

We can be living mainly in this perception or moving in and out but as a collective we have to move through 4D first. We are, but there's still work to do to reach critical mass.

The other false information I hear is, if you are a spiritual entrepreneur or spiritual being holding a sacred mission, that means you must live in poverty. These could be called spells and acts of sabotage, attacks against the sacred mission holders. This has been the way for many, many generations and it's time to say, "enough".

In the beginning, I didn't see all the paths that would assist me in my awakening, or even who I was here to serve, but that slowly unfolded. There are many levels of waking up, more than I first realised, but I kept trusting in something that felt more real than all of this.

We are taught that money is how we find value in ourselves. Mainstream society and information still focus on materialism, using marketing as a tool of greed and competition. The message it sends assumes people are aiming at being worshiped, or envied, which is a complete inversion of what is helpful and healing. It feels like force and pressure to keep up with the messages we are given, which is going against what is meant to be. It creates stress, illness and relationship breakdowns. We can have our physical needs met with ease and freedom without it being related to fear.

Marketing or promotion's true purpose is really about bringing our divine gifts into the world. It happens as a result of our deepest intention to return to love and that energy flows into our message. It feels to me like the icing on the cake for the effort we have made, to let all the fear go. Living a life of intension, love, abundance and joy.

It's imperative that those who hear that primordial call of your sacred mission from within, listen, even if it's missing some clarity, that will come. The time has come to launch and fully ignite your mission. What we need to be clear about is there is no more waiting for something to happen in the future. The energy supporting this is now. There has never been a time like it. This is the time to unfold your sacred purpose which is vital to wellbeing overall.

I don't know about you, but I didn't come to earth to live a meagre life that lacks sacred respect, truth, honour, courage and justice.

I came here to express the love that I am and to create a New World that can give rise to universal and Galactic order once again, I suspect we all did at some level. We are bringing and anchoring what we have heard being coined as "Heaven on Earth" once again. I believe this is the birth right of Gaia and all who live here.

It's imperative that we allow our sacred mission to rise and move into it with full attention and intention. It doesn't have to mean full time. You are more ready than you might think you are. The universe will support you just as it has for me. It's ok to still be letting go of any blockages, to still have doubts. That's the process, removing blockages and opening to love. You are bringing that magic of yours into this realm more and more by trusting, by being who you came here to be. We've been waiting for this for eons and the waiting is over. You are here, you are ok, it's time.

I'd like to share with you, my recent journey of attracting another aspect of my own sacred mission. On occasion I rent my house through Airbnb and decided this year I would. I have let my Higher-Self lead me and found this year 2024 to be a hugely transforming year. I decided with how I was feeling, rather than going away, I wanted to stay locally while my house was occupied. I received a booking for 6 nights which was the only time I opened up. Having my dates set, I went onto a community Facebook page and offered to house sit during this time. Now the odds are probably slim to match my criteria with an available house in my coastal town during holiday season and on top of that it was close to Christmas. Most people had already made their plans. The next day after my post I received an offer to house and pet sit for the exact dates I required.

When the house owner and I met, to sort out the details, something happened. We felt instantly at ease with each other, almost like this was a deja-vu. This can mean a couple of things; that our souls are destined to meet at this time to create something together or to support each other to align to 5D consciousness or both. In time our path will tell us. We cannot teach or share what we don't own so often these deja-vu meetings are to help us align to our life's path.

Stepping up to a new level requires us to be walking our talk. It's not about being perfect but it is about being conscious. This level of soul support can include triggering each other, which can be challenging. However, the challenge is not ever the trigger, it is the resistance to owning the limited belief or wound or to letting go of resistance.

This feels like the missing piece of my mission and regardless of who creates this with me, it feels like another wake up to my souls calling. The focus is to awaken the highest expression of each soul's mission. To shift from knowing to embodying your divine essence in every aspect of life. To step into the flow of 5D abundance so you can live your divine mission and make a powerful impact in the world.

I'm constantly amazed how this book has become the Jumanji board game. As I write each chapter, I am living it. I started noticing that early on but now as I'm readying it for my beautiful editor, there is no denying it. It might be the power of the words and the energy behind them. I am living this book, chapter by chapter. It's as if I am embodying all that I write about and gaining deeper and deeper insights. See what you notice. I trust there is a divine purpose beyond adding to this book and I look forward to uncovering that.

Love, like all things, begins with self. Rather than using the words success or wealth that have been tied to a control system of money, let's use the words self-worth because that is energy. *When a sacred mission holder doesn't have full trust or respect for themselves first, then they are not able to see their total and entire value, and this affects their entire mission.*

If we know we are here to co-create a whole new world connecting back to our origin, then building what is nothing short of a galactic civilization again is the intention. One with the connection of true God Source consciousness energies of the Divine. *We really don't have time to mess around and allow others to break down our self-worth energies any longer.* This affects our energy and that affects everything we are and do. So, looking after yourself is in the best interest of everyone. Choosing yourself is one of the most valuable things you can do on this journey to wholeness.

If we want to be all of who we are, we must relearn what it means to truly love ourselves and have mutual honour and respect for ourselves. As we heal and embrace our deeper self, we are drawn away from materialism, external gratification, old relationships that don't value us, and towards a simple life. We come home to ourselves and that is more than enough.

Self-love is essential to ascension, if we don't embody self-love we cannot love or be loved. Self-worth is a boundary; it's the line you draw that says this is who I am and this is how I deserve to be treated. It's the voice that speaks up and says I will not shrink to make you feel comfortable; I will not dim my light to make yours seem brighter. This voice is sometimes quiet and sometimes silent but always strong.

Here is the paradox of self-worth- the moment you stop seeking it from others, the moment you anchor it firmly within yourself the world begins to respond differently. People begin to see you as you see yourself, they reflect back the value you already possess. But by then it no longer matters because you are no longer waiting for their validation.

Self-worth is not about arrogance or ego; it's not about demanding attention or adoration. It is quiet, steady and unyielding. It is the foundation upon which you stand. The unshakable belief that you are enough. Not because of what you do or what you achieve but simply because you exist. And when you truly embrace that something extraordinary happens, you stop chasing after those who cannot see your worth. You stop settling for crumbs when you deserve the feast. You stop apologizing for who you are.

Instead, you begin to attract people, opportunities and experiences that align with your true value. *You begin to live not as someone waiting to be chosen but as someone who has already chosen themselves.* Hold onto that, even when it feels fragile, even when its challenged. Hold onto it with your whole heart because it's the most precious thing you have. It's the light that will guide you and the anchor that will steady you. It's the truth that will set you free.

It's time to be a guardian of your personal value. When we take a self-esteem hit, it feels like putting a lock on our full potential and our true calling. Let's dive into these techniques to mend self-worth wounds and unravel the consequences of not owning your true worth. Let's unveil the alchemy that kindles the flame of self-worth, thus empowering your quest in the most epic way possible.

We are the microcosm of the macrocosm, that is the responsibility we took on. We must let go of anything that holds us back. You can do anything you set your mind to, anything else is limitation.

When we walk the line of having sacred respect for ourselves, we begin to see that we didn't ever have to tolerate things that take our self-worth away. Healing our wounds around our self-worth allows us to align around the how and why of our powerfully creative process. Here are 3 steps that you can use:

INCONVENIENT CONSCIOUSNESS

Step 1) Self-worth has nothing whatsoever to do with financial worth. These two things are not connected. Your soul's worth has nothing to do with this false prison system controlling mechanism called money.

As you peel away your worth from being equal to what's in the bank and are no longer tied to money, you begin to see your value and worth as being far more than that. Your value is your magnificent light that has been brought into physicality or matter.

There is a sacred purpose within you and there's a reason why you're here, even if you are not totally clear about what it is. If you are reading this, you are already holding, or perhaps even living, your sacred mission. You're doing it, or maybe on the verge or even just considering, your possibilities. Trust and surrender, there's nothing to do, it will simply unfold.

Perhaps you're ready to refresh because you've been through a shift recently. It is likely evolving as you are. You know that feeling when things begin to feel a little lighter for a while. Perhaps it's because this is reminding you that you have worth, not only here but in many other dimensions as we are multi-dimensional beings. You are respected for your courage just to be here at this time, you are revered, supported and loved more than you could imagine.

I want to talk about how we make change in our lives. The brain is one area of our body that builds synapses and pathways that develop from repetitive thoughts and behaviours. The brain and the mind are different, in that the mind works through the brain. The mind refers to our ability to instigate beliefs, recognise feelings and engage in physical activity. The brain on the other hand refers to the physical organ in our head that supports these functions.

When we want to change our behaviour in this example towards self-love and value, we can assist this process in many ways. In this case, I'm going to offer a process through the use of mantras.

Sometimes these changes in our brain happen instantaneously and sometimes they are progressive. For example, when one of my clients takes part in a quit smoking session, generally it takes just one or two sessions. Other times for example, a belief that has been with them most of their lives or longer, the change is progressive. It's really up to the individual and their intentions. Here is the mantra for self-worth: "My self-worth and true worth is what I bring through the power of my soul. My uniqueness and I are precious beyond words. While they are connected to everyone and everything, are at the same time mine to own."

If we're not emotionally connected to money, it doesn't mean it's not important. Unfortunately, at the moment we live in a false prison and money, is a crutch for living. What we can do is change the way we see money, our perception of it and look at it, as an exchange of energy.

Step 2) How much of a *wake* are you creating with your passion as you drive your sacred mission boat? No matter what stage you are at, are you allowing it to create ripples or waves? Have you considered how many lifetimes it has taken for you to be at this place?

How much value are you giving this expression of your soul? Are you allowing this inner knowing to grow into what it needs to be, to find the place in your life it deserves? Are you going deep and moving with intention and consistency as you drive this sacred mission? If not now, when? Because this is not a dress rehearsal. We are here for this.

INCONVENIENT CONSCIOUSNESS

We're not really talking about a boat- it's your true purpose for being here at this time- a sacred mission yacht. Up until now, the wake of our missions has been centred around money, and it has gone as far as it can, but we can switch the lens. We can look at this to see all things as energy, that we either hinder or that we powerfully cultivate and create. When we are riding our SM yacht with intention and being consistent in how we show up, the wake of the yacht *includes* money that follows your mastery.

The difference is, you are not focused on the wake of money. *You are focused on your mission and serving others. You are focused on strategies and who you are showing up as. That drives your SM yacht. You are not in it for the money, but for the humans including yourself. For the animals, the earth and for the highest good of all in this realm and beyond. That creates abundance and bliss for you and all.*

When you are hyper focused and living your unique magic with grace, ease, and absolute intention, with the help of your creative power within, everything begins to fall into place, lines up and harmonises. It's you flipping your lens to see money is just following your energy.

Here you are exchanging your value from being about money and beginning to value who you are and what you have to give. Valuing your time, your energy, your creative powers, your uniqueness. Others invest in your guidance, your service or product because *"you" bring value to them.*

When you focus on giving value for money, which is the old way, it takes your focus away. This focus will add to what you create and how you serve. Synergies that have a ripple effect flow out and back to you. We can create abundance by serving in this way. Making material things sacred is not real, it's empty and more of the old

3D way. Most of us have seen through that. What is real and sacred are the bonds of connection that are held within all things. When you serve from the sacred heart within you, you are served back and everything finds balance. It is work, it takes focus, clarity and intention but it's worth it. This is grounding our New Earth.

Step 3) Focus on true value and only value and remember your uniqueness. Value needs to be translated into this energy exchange. When you focus on the value you are bringing, it changes the way you see what you are doing.

Instead of seeing things as products or services, start seeing them as your work as the sacred mission it is. The energy exchange is the value you're providing to those you are here to assist and serve. The most magnificent thing that you are bringing is a value that no one in this entire world can bring- it's your uniqueness. Even if there are others that do the same thing that you do, at the foundation they will do it differently. The best thing about you is that you are here to bring your essence into what you are here to do.

Your uniqueness is based on your values, upbringing, journeys of lifetimes, quests and your mission at hand. ***There is no one here on earth or in any aspect of creation exactly like you.*** *No one will ever see things the same way you see them, through your eyes, that holds immense value.*

When you truly know your uniqueness and value, it changes the way you show up in the world. You begin to see the value that only you can provide and this changes everything. This is what self-esteem, self-worth, self-love is based on. This becomes the icing on the sacred mission cake, when you can see through a whole new lens.

You see your uniqueness, your magic, unleashing of your divine gifts. Nothing in the world can stop you.

This world needs your magic, yet to some people the 3D life has become a distraction. But you can break free if you choose to. This world needs all of us who came here with sacred missions to ensure we are doing our unique mastery and pouring out the greatest and most sacred service that we are here to bring.

We have come here to break the low and vile magic of the negative factions that keep humanity small. They don't deserve any more space in this book other than to say they have trapped us in what could be called a slave or death system for long enough. It's time to live, to change the world by unleashing your unique mission with all of your essence and let us all show the world what true action looks like.

Every one of us has an ingredient to add to the making of this New World and every ingredient matters. A chocolate cake just wouldn't be the same without chocolate, or flour or eggs. We really can become the change we want to see in this world. Action that is heart motivated, where we all serve under this umbrella of kindness and compassion. Together we can show this planet the power of collective heart-centred impact that is driven by love.

Love has always been at the core of our activities on planet earth, even in the darkest of times. We can see these times were helping us to know what we don't want, (rather than being a negative experience or a mistake) and that makes us clearer in knowing what we do want. It's often those extremely challenging times that encourage us to come together and to reach deeply within ourselves to find our strength and true nature. Everything does serve a purpose.

This too is the purpose for the challenges ahead of us. There may be some challenges on the horizon knowing about the nature of evolution. Perhaps there will be an earth rift, environmental happenings, more wars or other significant events. These will mirror, in some ways, the collective struggle: as above, so below, as within, so without. In history, when things have been a great struggle for humankind, the only way we got through was by coming together. These challenges are the collective fear when it forges into form, that which we would rather not see. How else will we address the behaviours that are not working if we cannot see them? How else will we let go of separation, other than needing each other and coming together?

During these times ahead, we may not always have the every-day comforts that we have become attached to and reliant on, but this will serve to help us become unattached and discover more of our true selves. The saying, "Everything happens for a reason" gives all of these events meaning. This is not designed to trigger fear but if it is within you, it may do just that, so you can own it and release it. Ask yourself, "What am I afraid of?" then you will know what is holding you back. It can only be let go by acknowledging its existence. Life is designed to allow you to be free and see the bigger picture, that all things have a place and serve you, humanity and the universe in some way.

You are always supported and loved by the Divine and all of life. You are brought into form for a purpose- for love to transpire between, and amongst, you. When you remember this, love will forge through your choices and your actions, thoughts and emotions. We create divinity within the bonds of strength between us.

The love that transpires shall grow as we become inter-reliant and inter-dependant, loving ourselves and all. Love is leading us home, to oneness, to our New World.

Love is such a force even in this 3D reality, that there are more than 100 million love songs recorded, and a similar number of movies and poems written on the subject. It really is everywhere we go. The well-known and watched scene from terminal three, Heathrow airport arrival lounge in the movie "Love Actually" comes to mind when I think about love. This scene is about welcoming home loved ones, where people are showing each other how much they mean to them, regardless of who is looking on. They are unapologetically and bravely showing love. When you witness that, how do you feel? Have you wondered why it feels so good? Could it be that in that moment you are witnessing the truth of who you are?

When we feel unhappy to any degree, it is due to our resistance to life, and life is love, therefore this disconnects us from love and the truth of who we are. We sometimes call this depression, sadness, hopelessness or loneliness. It feels awful so we have been programmed to think that something must be wrong, so we do something about it. We resist it by taking drugs for example to push it down or numb us from it temporarily. But it will persist until we own it, lean into it because it is information that is calling for our attention. This is the perfection of the universe. Designed for us to notice what isn't working so we can be free.

It's always moving us towards our highest good and greatest joy. Nature's laws want us to be happy and free, not temporarily or inauthentically but genuinely and permanently free. Only your personal journey can create this for you, if, or when you surrender to it.

When you hold onto the past and let that affect you in this current time, you are then out of alignment with your true self or higher-self. As a result, you feel negative emotions. Holding on or reliving the past, is resisting your life in the present. This is resistance. This is a bit like getting food poisoning from a restaurant and asking for some take away, so you can have a little reminder of how awful it was when it first happened. Sounds crazy, right?

Many people say they do this rehashing, to remind themselves of something they don't wish to repeat. And if they revisit it over and over, this will somehow ensure that they don't repeat it. This is not the case, and I'll explain why- when you were young and you touched a hot stove, you didn't need to do it over and over again to know "That hurts. Its hot. Don't do that again". Touching a hot stove is painful but as a child, experiencing it once was enough. Ruminating over the past is the old way of being and it can only be done within the mind, so take back control of your life and choose your thoughts with care. I heard a simple reminder of this recently- "too much thinking makes you sad". So simple and yet so wise.

The reason this repetition is unnecessary is because our unconscious mind is wired to keep us safe and will keep track of any experiences that cause us angst or problems. Our body gives us a feeling that assists us by reflecting the event to serve as a warning, such is the wisdom of the human being. You remember what a burn feels like, even when you are not being burnt.

The key to happiness is staying aligned to your higher-self. How we know when we are out of alignment with our higher-self is when we are out of the stream of joy, wellbeing and freedom. It feels yuck and is designed that way, so we don't hang around in that place any longer than necessary. When we are out of alignment, we have lowered our vibration and the results are feeling heavy, sad, anxious or any one of the fear-based negative emotions that lets us know this is not who we are. That's why our feelings are so valuable. Ultimately, they guide us back to who we really are.

INCONVENIENT CONSCIOUSNESS

We attract energy to ourselves, that are directly related to our thoughts. As a rule, positive thoughts create positive feelings and negative thoughts create negative feelings. This experience is not to punish us or even a judgement of us by the universe or the Divine, as judgement is man-made. We are given free will and loved in whatever way we choose to use it. The purpose of this is to bring our attention to the ability we have to create our reality. That's how valuable that awareness is. You are a creator spark, creating creation, every moment of your life.

It shows us what may have been or is currently unconscious to us, so then if we choose to, we can bring it into our conscious awareness and make a correction towards what we want.

My sense of the world's problems stem from being disconnected from love, through the disconnection we experience from our true self. If we believe in the old paradigm that we are separate from each other and from our creator, then that separation flows through ourselves and into our lives. Our ego-self has preferences for those we love and those we don't. Even those of us who are choosing love consciously can still have areas of disconnection in our lives while we are in the process of letting go of the 3D reality. Waking up has many layers.

We have preferences for so many things, judging one thing as being better than another and feeling we must follow these thoughts and instructions because we will be happier if we do. For example, how you feel about a certain suburb or town, the way you celebrate Christmas (if at all), how you feel about a particular culture or race of people, age of people or a particular animal. You may love or dislike certain places, people or things.

Many of us love to shop in one place because we feel good there and reject other places because they don't look the right way or the people there are not the way we prefer.

We can love those people who are nice to us but when it comes to "difficult" people, we choose to withdraw our love from them, telling ourselves stories that justify our actions. We can remove ourselves from harmful relationships while still loving the people in them.

Many masters have visited our planet to speak of love. Jesus showed us how he spent time with people who were feared and rejected by most of the population. They had leprosy and were called Lepers. He showed us, not only did he love them personally, he loved every part of them, even the Leprosy. That is unconditional love, love that doesn't separate.

Separation can sneak up on us, perhaps looking as innocent as a preference but it leads to disconnection which closes our heart and shuts off love. Opening your heart is a capacity you have, and you must open your heart more completely if you want to have this understanding - loving awareness of another's embodiment. This allows you to perceive them gentler, with greater understanding, with compassion and with connection.

The only reason we don't love the darkness or evil on the planet, is we are afraid of it, which is true for anything we don't love. We are afraid that it will affect us, that we'll catch it and it will drag us under. This fear is the same as other f-e-a-r-s, (False Evidence Appearing Real) it's a story we have either created or, through repetition, come to believe and is based on nothing else.

A story is a group of thoughts when you break it down. Just thoughts and they have no power unless we give it to them. When you are full of your own light, strong and sure, nothing will match that. Only those old and unacknowledged things you have within you can stick so there is nothing to fear.

That is the reason I can be there for my clients, because I have faced those parts of myself that they come to the session to heal. This allows me to be there for them without any fear and without it sticking to me. If you are healed, have done the work, you can love everyone and everything. You can bring it into your heart knowing you are whole and sovereign. You can love it, whatever it is because it's a part of humanity, a part of the spectrum of what we are so courageously experiencing. As the illusion dissolves, you discover that there is nothing to fear and that's the difference that makes all the difference.

When we entertain fear, we push love away. When fear dissolves, we reconnect with the love that we are. We welcome love in, which is becoming sovereign because we know we create our own life from our place of perception: *I know I will not become something that is other than me when I stand fully in my own light.* That is the shift. I've noticed in my life as an Empath, if I don't stand fully in my own light, then I will spend a lifetime playing out other people's wounded selves. I did that for most of my earlier life at least until more recently. Empowered living is honouring your awareness of the energy coming toward you and setting boundaries to support that.

Some Empaths find earth more than they can manage due to the constant experience of living in separation. Due to our sensitivity many of us go into hermit mode and spend large amounts of time physically alone. We are extremely loving and thrive on connection so this can be painful. Many people don't understand us so exclude us from many events and gatherings which feeds these feelings of separation. It feels completely foreign and very painful to a being who knows oneness, because it goes against who we know ourselves to be. Through this intense pain compassion and the memory of oneness, we are destined to be brought back to ourselves. Standing so full of your own light that nothing can get in the way, is living fully and the life we were intended to live.

This is an evolved state of being and in this state, boundaries can be expressed through empowerment and love. Jesus demonstrated boundaries when he removed the traders from his place of prayer. The difference was this was done with assertiveness, not anger.

Anger is an emotion of disempowerment. We cannot lose ourselves when we are in a state of unity, where our masculine and feminine energies are balanced and united, being full of our own light is the shift.

As you head into the final chapter, I'd like to share the gifts of facing and releasing fear that my life has shown me and embracing love as a way of life. I share this, so that it will encourage you to keep going and to find trust and patience in your own process.

This shift that evolves in a natural progression leads to the new world or 5D. We really are blessed to be here at this time. It is an experience like no other. Something extraordinary occurs in this evolution of the human when we return to unity, becoming a part of everything and everyone. It really is the adventure of our lifetimes.

Wherever you are on this path is perfect for you and the world around you and you will undertake unique symptoms and experiences. But as you progress and return to this unity consciousness or perception of love, you are still living on earth but are no longer at the effects of all the 3D drama.

This is because you have moved timelines from the Karmic path to the Dharmic path. It will be different for each of us and will most likely happen progressively. As you ground your shift you are in a state of self-love where you are able to fully stand in your power, in your light and in your truth always. You may come in and out from time to time until the new synapses and pathways are built, until your vibration has settled.

Love is where you settle, from inside out and then it becomes everything. Every thought, every vision, every sound, every decision, every action, every intention and every feeling. Is that not what we have been searching for, the life of our dreams?

CHAPTER 8 QUESTIONS:

A) What is your definition of love?

B) Where in your life is love a motivator?

C) What role does love play in your life?

D) What value if any, can you see in understanding the love languages?

E) Which love language or languages do you relate to? How does or will knowing this affect your relationships?

F) Do you see room for change in our current earthy reality? What are the changes you'd like to see?

G) Can you identify some preferences you have that lead to separation?

H) When or where are you out of alignment in your life?

I) Where are you in alignment in your life?

J) What are your thoughts and feelings about creating a New World together?

K) What is something you can do to raise your vibration, knowing it benefits you and the entire planet?

CHAPTER 9

THE MEANING OF LIFE LEADING US HOME!

Here you are at this last chapter. You've stayed the distance, and I want to acknowledge you for that. Take a moment and thank **you**, for finishing what you started. This knowledge is not for the faint of heart. I see every single human as a master who demonstrates courage almost every day of their lives. All of us have shown great bravery just living on planet earth.

We've explored the nature of consciousness. We've looked at this opportunity of shifting, growing and evolving into a New World and asked, what is awakening? We've considered how the universe is kind and wise and how life is always happening for us and through us, not to us. We've taken a deeper dive into being a highly sensitive person, talked about shifting dimensions and the nature of our soul. We have explored the power you have to manifest your life, gone a little deeper into your very nature- which is love- and, finally, we are here. The subject in front of us now is a summary of all that you have travelled through while reading this book.

Have you ever asked yourself, "What is all of this for?" Or "What is the meaning of life?" It's probably questioning most conscious people have pondered at some time in their lives.

As human beings most of us experience innate urges, intuitive promptings, thoughts, feelings or confirmations, synchronicities, even behaviours, feelings and senses which seem to go beyond the human condition. The demonstration of inner directives to care for each other, often shown in events such as natural disasters, have been seen all around the globe since the beginning of time.

When us humans are living true to our nature, we innately know of our oneness. Have you ever had a thought of someone and soon afterwards they call you or you see them unexpectedly? What about children and how they are innately loving, inclusive and compassionate. And unless they've experienced something traumatic and it closed their heart, are naturally drawn to nature and animals. They often have invisible friends or speak of seeing spirits or loved ones who have passed over. They are still in a pure state from which we came. As we transcend this current reality and return to this pure state, these spiritual happenings increase, and we can access other realms and new information which is part of our expansion.

When we are prepared to do the work on ourselves, to go with our own life's flow, our path opens up for us and to us. From time to time most of us will come across resistance in its many forms, within ourselves and others. Resistance to acceptance of what life is showing us, to what we are experiencing. At times protecting ourselves from a past event or following our ego's preference rather than life's flow.

This resistance shows up to inform us of where our attention is needed, what needs to be let go of and to remind us that life is happening for us, not to us. It shows us that all of life has a part to play and will lead us if we surrender to it, to our highest good and greatest joy.

There are aspects of our bodies, our consciousness, our planet and elements within and on Earth, that are designed to assist us at a greater level to progress through the destined changes of this shift.

We are given a greater level of assistance than we may have been aware of until now, not only here, but as I've spoken about throughout the universe. This planet Gaia herself has many energetically significant and Sacred places that support her and her inhabitants. Many of these have been recognised by Indigenous communities around the world and are now being acknowledged by the wider community. Such places as Uluru, Stonehenge, Mount Sinai, Glastonbury Tor, Golden Temple, Jerusalem, Buddha Stupa, Machu Picchu and Mt Shasta. Many people are drawn to such places beyond what their conscious mind understands. If you have ever had the opportunity to experience the energy of such a place you will know what I mean.

I had such an experience myself in January 2020 when I was in the Northern Territory of Australia at Uluru. I had been at "Cosmic Consciousness Conference" where we listened to many key speakers discussing the many aspects of spirituality, this unique time on the planet and the universe. We were also there to help activate Uluru.

The story was told by the First Nations Elders of how many thousands of years earlier our original people, the First Nations Australians attempted to activate the rock but were interrupted by nature and told it was not the right time. During my stay in the Northern Territory near Uluru, I visited the rock several times and was in awe of the majestic energy of the site. This particular day I was walking with a new friend who I had met at the conference named Nick. It was a typical January day in the Northern Territory, around 48C and very still. So even for someone like me who loves the warm weather, I think it was fair to say, it was hot.

After walking around the rock for a couple of hours we decided to head back to the bus. During our return we caught up with the driver when he suddenly turned to us and said, "Don't come with me. I'll bring the bus back to you". The interesting thing is that I had been having urges to continue on the track and walk ahead rather than turn off where the bus was parked. This was one of those confirmations of my feelings, that life sometimes gives us.

Together, Nick and I kept walking forward and soon came to a place that was fenced off and known as "The Women's Birthing Place". As the name suggests, this area was only for women so we could only view it from a distance. The original people referred to some places as being just for men; Men's Business and this one was for women; Women's Business. We were both being drawn to this site like a moth to a flame. We walked in silence and stopped immediately in front of this sacred site.

The tour guides who were First Nations People explained the rock was not sacred as is often reported, however, the site itself is sacred and is deeply respected by their people. I stood there in front of the birthing place which could not be better described other than sacred. There was a silence, a feeling of peace and reverence surrounded us. It felt as though I had stepped into another realm of consciousness.

As we stood there in front of the birthing area, a beautiful light of a golden white colour shone down like a beam from the sky. It was breathtaking and felt as though it was something quite significant. It was like witnessing liquid sunlight and it not only guided us where to look but moved us deeply. The feeling was pure love. It brought me to tears. Nick explained that he received information as we stood there- he heard that this was the portal of all souls entering earth. I felt privileged just to be there. If you ever feel drawn to visit a sacred site, I'd love to hear about it in our community page.

The law of attraction is at play everywhere, all the time. Nick and I were drawn to this place and maybe our energies of male/female were of assistance in some way. I guess, we may never know, we just followed our life's path. How we resonate, or our personal vibration attracts vibrations of the same resonance. Like attracts like. Birds of a feather flock together, are all good examples of this. The inhabitants of an environment will resonate with their environment. This seems to be a physical example of our connectedness. One example of this is planet Earth, how it is approximately seventy-three percent water, the same as we humans are. Water is one example of the wisdom of our elements that is now beginning to be revealed. Water is evolving, as is our planet.

Dr Masaru Emoto's experiments on water molecules as seen in the movie "What the bleep" and his book "The Message from Water" are some examples of this wisdom. He freezes droplets of water then examines them under a darkfield microscope that has photographic capabilities. His work proves that our consciousness, our intent, and our sounds physically change the molecular structure of water.

For example, the crystals formed with water when introduced to words of fear and anger changed to dark and small, with no apparent structure, almost mould-like and unhealthy. They looked similar to water taken from contaminated water in the Yodo River in Japan. In contrast when water molecules were introduced to expressions of love and gratitude, they became similar to the clean water taken from Mount Cook Glacier in New Zealand. They were beautifully formed and looked healthy, clear, large and rainbow in colour. Water is the source of life and something our planet or ourselves could not survive without.

Water in its purist form has the appearance of light. My feeling is water holds information as all light does. Have you ever sat by the ocean or a river and gained some helpful information? I have and still do from time to time. It holds history and knowledge, and it supports our life like nothing else. I often talk to my water and give it my gratitude and love before ingesting it. This could become a source of curiosity as we evolve as a species and could perhaps even be a source of wisdom to help guide us. It certainly reflects our connection to all things: when we are lost, unclear and filled with resistance, so too do our bodies of water reflect this.

I trust and hope as we cleanse our energy and raise our consciousness and vibration so too will the water ways on our planet become clear. First Nations Australians looked after the water ways of our country for more than sixty thousand years and after only two hundred years of white man living here, we cannot drink our water without treatment. I prefer to use a filter, so I know what I am taking into my body.

In order to understand our human experience a little deeper, let's take a look at one part of our human vessel as a tool of progress. It hasn't received the attention or value that is deserves but it speaks to our higher purpose and the magnificence of this life. I'm speaking about the Pineal gland. It's sometimes referred to as our third eye as it's in this area although slightly higher. This gland is found near the centre of the brain, directly behind the middle point of our eyebrows and unlike other brain parts, and more like the heart, it is not paired as there is only one.

The function most commonly linked to the Pineal gland is secretion of melatonin which regulates our sleep and wake cycles. This gland is light sensitive and regulates our biological clock. Darkness stimulates the Pineal gland to release melatonin which controls your sleep cycles. Along with our food intake, stress levels, physical activities and social environment, it helps regulate our Circadian rhythms. This affects our sleep, body temperature, hormones, appetite and other bodily functions. So perhaps you can see why I'm focusing on this particular gland. But wait, there's more ...

The Pineal gland has a greater role to play in our development as a species in both metaphysical and spiritual dimensions. It is understood to be the gateway to our spiritual connection, to our higher-self and to each other. The Hindu's connect the third eye area to our intuition and clairvoyance. The physical eyes and third eye are indirectly connected. Jesus said, "The eye is the lamp of the body and if the eye is clear, your body will be filled with light." This is believed to relate to the eye of intuition (Pineal gland) and seeing things clearly and in truth. Research shows, (I encourage you to do your own) that this gland has photo receptors, and it's lined with similar tissue to the retina. It also has the same wiring to the visual cortex in the brain, as the eyes do. There are tiny floating crystals in the Pineal gland that vibrate when under pressure and give off light. This is called piezoluminescence and is well documented in many research papers.

Now that we have shone a light on the Pineal gland, lets look at how we can introduce some new behaviours that support this valuable gland that will support us in being a new human moving forward:

1) Fluoride, found in most Australian water and many other places, is known to calcify the Pineal gland so sourcing pure water is important. There is historical documentation explaining the restriction of human potential by using fluoride in our water as far back as the Nazi party who added it to the drinking water of ghettos and prison camps.

2) Rather than doing research, human experimentation in these camps showed that fluoride makes people more docile and subservient as well as sterilizing them. Interesting how many young people struggle to conceive and need more intervention for reproduction than any time in history.

3) Keep your attention on your third eye regularly: where your attention goes, energy flows and that's how it functions more efficiently.

4) Yoga philosophy talks about the simple practice of sitting in a meditative state or stillness, closing down your eyes and rolling your physical eyes towards the centre of your eyebrows. Stay in this position for as long as is comfortable. This is not done for a particular outcome, rather to become curious as to where it leads you.

5) Light management: The Pineal gland becomes active when the light goes down. Nature guides us to be active during the day and to rest at night. Much of our lives are currently out of rhythm and our health reflects that, using bright lights at night continues our activity. Make it a practice to put your screens away as you dim your lights one hour before bed.

Eye exercises for supporting this gland:

1) Look at your palm then move your gaze to a distant object and bring it back and forth 30-50 times. Rotate your eyes in a full circle and then back the other way. Rotate your eyes looking at your shoulders, left then right.

2) Look at the tip of your nose and hold it, then look at the centre of your eyebrows or the Pineal gland area. We exercise most of our bodies so why not our eyes? Exercising your eyeballs keeps them in a healthy state. This also helps keep the Pineal gland active and healthy.

3) Most people are unaware of how this gland can be a physical connection to the vastness of our human nature. Fortunately, this is a time where the veil of consciousness is thinning which is uncovering many truths, wisdoms and information such as this. Which can help us make sense of our lives and the path before us.

Hindu philosophy refers to deities that speak to the three pillars of existence. Each referring to one cosmic function. Brahma the creator; Vishnu the preserver, and Shiva the destroyer. It says this is the process of life and we need all three in order to sustain balance and keep moving forward. If things were only created and destroyed but not preserved, Shiva would destroy everything. If things were only created and preserved and not destroyed, we would rapidly become overwhelmed and overcrowded with everything, everywhere. If we only preserved and destroyed and didn't create, in time nothing would exist. This shows us that rather than the components of life being separate from each other, (which has been the story of the old 3D world), in truth everything is connected and interdependent.

Now let's look at "leading us home". Where is our true home and is it physical or spiritual? Human kind, even from a very early age build cubbies and homes as a place of shelter, to retreat and feel safe in. In a physical sense, the ideal home is a place where we experience a sense of being safe and in charge of your environment. At this stage on the planet, it's a place we refer to that gives us every opportunity to be at ease and in alignment with our best self.

In a spiritual sense, when I think of home, there are times when I connect to my higher-self or my soul and, at other times, I connect through my heart centre. I'm absolutely sure this process of finding your home is a personal path and cannot be rushed or done by someone else. Not by a guru, a religious or spiritual group, nor a healer or doctor of any kind. Just like awakening and conscious evolution, this is personal, and its journey and destination are uncovered, rather than planned or controlled. In fact, the journey reveals all you need to know along the way, to arrive consciously at this golden desire of contentment.

I mentioned earlier about my suspicion that the seed of all grief on our planet is the limited belief that we are separate from everything and everyone. We have been conditioned to believe, this place I refer to as home and the energy that resides there- Source energy, the beginning and ending of everything, is something that is apart from ourselves.

As I wrote these words being an empath, a huge wave of what felt like collective sadness swept over me, so perhaps this is the truth or at least an aspect of it. Our feelings don't lie. But the question remains what is, and where is, our home?

Many of us have heard the saying, there is nothing new in the universe. I also doubt there is any original thought. This becomes particularly evident when we receive guidance from Spirit. In fact, the belief in ownership is really a 3D concept. I'm sure in our new world there will be no patents or intellectual property. An example of this is how First Nation Australians say, "This country is not owned by us, but we are the caretakers of it."

With this in mind and due to my curiosity, I'd like to share a process (while making it ours in my unique way) that I came across that helped me know, in a spiritual sense, what it feels like to be home.

We can call it "Surrendering into the hands of the Divine:"

This process will take around 30 minutes. When you are ready, go ahead and continue:

When you are in a comfortable quiet position, where you will not be disturbed, close your eyes.

Become aware of your breath, breathing slowly and evenly. You can breathe in for the count of four and out for the count of four, ideally, just a light shallow type of breath.

Slow focused breathing is a tremendously healthy activity. It slows your mind and helps regulate your nervous system. Notice a wave of relaxation that I refer to as the alpha wave, flowing across your scalp as it relaxes, your forehead, smoothing the muscles as it flows down around your temples, those tiny muscles around your eyes, let them go and your eyelids feel heavier and heavier.

Now notice your cheeks relaxing and all those muscles around your mouth, even your tongue is dropping away from the roof as your jaw relaxes.

This wave of relaxation is now flowing down your throat and neck and washing across your shoulders. Feel those shoulders sinking down. All the tension, any concerns or thoughts are washing away. This alpha wave is now flowing down your arms to the forearms, all the way down to your fingertips. Those arms become very, very heavy.

This wave of relaxation is now starting to travel down your back, relaxing the shoulder blades and trickling down the spinal cord, vertebrae by vertebrae.

Sending out a message to the entire nervous system to relax, let go, there's not a care in the world at this moment. It flows down to the lower back and relaxes your buttocks muscles. Your entire back let's go as you continue to sink down, deeper and deeper.

This alpha wave now flows down into your chest and allows your chest to sink deeper, comfortably breathing easy and naturally. It continues flowing through all of your internal organs, relaxing them and allowing them to work at their healthiest and most relaxed state.

It continues down into your abdomen, relaxing the muscles so your stomach only does what it absolutely has to do right now. Your hips relax, your pelvis relaxes and you drift down deeper and deeper. This relaxing wave now flows into your thigh muscles, the large muscles at the top of those legs become limp, loose and relaxed. Flowing through the knees back and front, shins and calf muscles as they soften too.

Your legs become very heavy. You can feel them sinking below the surface you're relaxing on. Those legs are feeling very heavy. Arms and legs are feeling heavy. Heavy as led. As if they don't want to move. They feel good just as they are. This wave continues as it flows through the ankles and out of the feet. Relaxing you completely.

Now I want to talk to your wise mind, your higher-self, who is always listening to me in this relaxed state. Imagine yourself in your current life. See, sense, imagine or feel yourself surrounded by your current circumstances, your job, your home, your relationships.

With the choices you've made, your emotional, mental and physical addictions. Imagine the path that is before you and all the stuff that is surrounding you. You are standing on this path surrounded by all the facets of your life and noticing how these feel.

Many great teachers believe that life is meant to feel light, be fun, joyous and flowing. The truth is if you are in alignment with yourself and your divine plan, contrast will still exist, but you will perceive it differently (contrast are things being strikingly different from what you desired). The contrast of a fine sunny day is a cold and windy one.

Way up above you in the distance, you sense a smooth road, a new road filled with new intentions. You have learnt a lot from this road you've been travelling on but as you've grown, you've also outgrown this old road. Now there is a lightness in your being as you understand the lessons your being taught. You transform everything to wisdom and love with relative ease, making everything quick and efficient. You are enjoying life, understanding that everything is a present for you, a gift, as you are the co-creator of your reality, not a victim of it.

In order for these new intentions to manifest as a part of your reality, you must understand and surrender to the greatest good. That is, without the often confined and limited reality when you see only a piece of the puzzle.

Source of all that is, has unlimited possibilities, infinite potential available to us with a broad and unbounded perspective of our life. Trust Source to lead you along the path which is in your highest good and the highest good of all concerned. There are reasons why things don't work out in your life as you originally planned. You can trust your higher-self who is always guiding you, and that Source, the Divine knows the best road for you to take.

Trust that the Divine knows you and is answering your every desire in ways that are in yours and everyone's best interest. So, right now, as you are standing on your path surrounded by aspects of your life. I want you to look up, way up high above you and feel this loving presence, see or sense a beautiful bright, warm light. From this light, see a hand reaching down to you. The hand of the Divine is being offered to you. If you choose to take it, reach up and grab hold of this loving hand. Allow it to lift you up. Allow this infinite loving presence to lift you onto a clear and uninterrupted path. See yourself standing next to Source as this divine and loving presence holds your hand and walks next to you.

On this path all things that are not necessary or dysfunctional have dropped away, leaving what is only in your best interest and highest good. This new path is clear and light. A luminescent path of golden light. On this path the Divine walks along side of you, holding your hand. You feel this support and direction in your life. It now feels like there is a great reason for your life and expression and how it actually expands the whole of the universe.

Your life is important and whatever you choose to do or has significance and meaning. You are expressing the light of the Divine in every moment. Whatever you choose, all is perfect and divine.

There is a sense of confidence building within you as you walk along this new path, side by side holding hands with the infinite Divine Source of all that is. You can feel the love Source has for you as it brings about your desires in natural and fulfilling ways.

It listens to your soul's deepest intention, dreams and desires and it knows you. This loving presence knows you better than you know yourself. It cares deeply about you and for you, and always wishes for you to feel good, fulfilled, happy, joyous and loved. For that is why you were created, an expression of love for the joy of existence.

You can feel trust growing within you as you spend time walking with the Divine. You can feel certainty and confidence as it brings you to that which you love and desire in the best possible way.

You can trust it to know the perfect way for you to receive what you've been asking for. Follow your intuition, recognise that what you have been given is in direct alignment with what you have been focused on. As you pay attention to what you have been asking for, it will appear. That is the way the universe receives your desires, through your focussed attention.

Take time to walk hand in hand with the creator, this infinite presence. Talk and listen or feel for your answers.

This direct communication between you and the Divine is always available to you and you will always be answered whether it's now or in the future. Be open to this guidance, this is our sovereign state of being where our answers come from within. Close this book for a while if you wish. Take some time here …

After time walking with the Divine, you decide with renewed trust that you will accept what comes to you as the gift that it is. Everything is helping you get closer to who you really are.

You gain wisdom from everything that presents itself in your life and you let the Divine guide you towards the highest good for all concerned. Then you surrender and trust this Divine Source to work in your life as you walk together side by side. Surprising and delighting you at every turn, showering you with abundance and joy. Always being present for you and with you.

Your path is bright and clear as you walk hand in hand with the Divine Source of all that is. Maintaining this infinite presence in you always. The hand that is always holding yours, collaborating with you to bring about your greatest dreams and desires.

Now I'm going to count you back up from that deep state, right back into your body and into the room you're in. One, feel the surface you are resting on, two, feel the air against your skin, three, you can take a deep breath and help yourself come back, four, notice your fingers moving and five, eyes open, wide awake, feeling good, really good, all the way back into your room.

I hope you enjoy using this script and process. When I did this exercise, it was quite life changing and I feel that it's because I've kept this connection strong by focusing on it. I consciously connect in this way often in my meditation or at yoga. I give my focus to the Divine; I feel the love and ask for guidance. I see it as a discipline and as I often say, I'm a work in progress and not perfect but perfectly me. The clarity and direction this brings to my life is extraordinary. Even with the challenges, actually it feels like it supports me especially through the challenges. I highly recommend it.

It seems like nature's guide post is simple; when it feels good and is doing no harm, then it is good for you.

So, as we draw closer to completing our time together, I want to share some tools I hope you find helpful. Most of you will have experienced supressing your feelings sometime in your life. We do this as a protection when our feelings are either negated, they seem too difficult to manage, judged or disrespected. We do this out of fear. To reconnect with feelings, I had suppressed as a child and even before that, was a big project. Personal examples can be useful to bring these words to life, so I'll talk about my own journey a little more.

I know everyone does their best with the knowledge they have at the time and I'm not parent or guardian bashing in any way but for the sake of this example: I'll use my childhood experience. Growing up, the messages I received were; you are wrong about your feelings, they are not what you think they are. No doubt this came from an overwhelmed person, however, it still had adverse effects. For example, if I said I felt sad, I was told, "No, you don't feel sad". If I felt scared, I was told, "No, you don't feel scared". I know now that this is a form of gaslighting, which creates feelings of confusion and disorientation, and we lose confidence in who we are. Our feelings are communication from our soul, our essence. Children naturally trust in them unless this trust is broken. What I made it mean back then was, I couldn't trust myself to know how I felt. As children we believe the messages we receive from significant people because that makes us feel safe. We innately know our feelings are a part of our essence, so I decided I couldn't trust myself, full stop.

And as life progressed, I continued to push my feelings down, all of them, down deep. Not only did I not trust my feelings, but I was completely confused because I've always had big feelings which added to my level of fear and separation.

I disconnected from myself because I couldn't trust who I thought I was. Exploring this in greater depth as my life progressed, I began to understand why I had no sense of self. I am eternally grateful for the understanding that my experience offered me and to all those who contributed to it. There is no greater lesson than experience.

My feelings are a part of me, and without them I am just going through the motions. I made my choices in my earlier life to that point of awakening, from a place of distrust of myself and from what I thought others wanted of me. This was the pattern that resulted from my past experiences. I feel deep gratitude for this experience, as difficult as it was to face because it has given me a firsthand experience of the struggles so many people face. I know how it feels to be what I think others want, rather than who I am, and the excruciating pain that loosing ourself causes.

This reconnecting with my feelings and, in essence my true self, took great courage. It is a path I am grateful for having taken. The way I did it was my journey- leaving my marriage, spending time in a "not cult" spiritual group and moving house over fifty times. There were other past wounds that I was healing along the way, but this really was at the core of everything. Pushing our feelings down must come to an end if we want to know ourselves, have direction, joy and passion in life. Our feelings are our guidance system and without them we are lost, and the purpose of our life is lost. My life taught me this. Our purpose or divine mission is known through our feelings, and that is why we seem so lost without them. The very reason for our life is a treasure held within our feeling body.

As we feel, we heal. There are many ways to accomplish healing, and the good news is the way us first wavers did it is no longer necessary. When you hold an intention, the universe will bring to you the most appropriate way to achieve that.

There was no pathway for this back then and it took absolute courage and dedication. I understand why some of us dropped out of our Third Dimensional life as I did; in order to find our way back and sadly, many didn't make it. This reminds me of this saying I heard: For everything to fall into place, firstly it must fall apart. Those of us who fought on, left our jobs, our families, our religious groups, our friends, anything we could do to make sense of this place. It took all we had to give, to just stay here. It took my entire focus to find a reason to go on but from this challenging time I developed great resilience and strength.

Almost every shift we achieved back in the 1990's right up until around 2019-2020 was cutting a path for the entire planet while healing our ancestors' wounds and our own. But that's what we signed up for, even if a little naïvely. Without the memory or information that we have today about our heritage, there was a part of me that knew- no matter what, this had to be done.

I'm eternally grateful for all that my path has offered and that, as a result of my early life I have a good understanding of feelings, and how to help others reclaim the courage to access and sit with their own. They are our compass, positive when we are fear-free and aligned, or negative when we are out of alignment and letting fear control us. Once we have let go of the resistance and the past, we can give our energy instead, to what we want more of. Because as creator sparks, whatever we think about, we bring about.

It has definitely become much faster to make a shift of recent times. Once the feeling is identified, it only needs to be felt, but I mean felt fully, for about 90 seconds and then see where it takes you. I'm not talking about major trauma; I'm talking about old wounds. Gone are the days of slogging through days, months, years of struggle, thank God/Goddess. Thank those who went out ahead and cut the path to make this time even just a little bit lighter for the next waves.

As human kind goes through this transformational shift, or Ascension you might also find the entire universe is with us and supporting us in all kinds of ways. Here is a hopefully uncomplicated big picture of the support we are receiving moving forward: from 2023 until 2026 planets are changing signs like never before. Currently we are going through the Photon Belt and light energy is pouring into our world. We are experiencing a great many solar flares. This has never happened before to this degree. The solar cycles, which is the cycle the suns magnetic field goes through, take approximately eleven years. In 2018 we didn't have a single M class flare and just last month we had thirteen. That's how different this time is.

We are talking about support from energy, physics, cosmology and astrology, then there are the prophecies such as the Hopi prophecy, talking about the significance of this time. But I think beyond all that data, most of us can feel it. We are becoming more psychically sensitive, more telepathic, more intuitive, more sensitive to our foods, to nature, even to each other. Perhaps sensitivity will become the new normal. When we see and acknowledge the support around us, we feel safe to choose to support our own life.

Choosing yourself is one of the most profound and difficult decisions a person can make yet it will, in time, lead you home. It's not merely a matter of indulgence or convenience. It is a radical act of courage that requires standing against the tide of expectations, obligations and deeply ingrained social norms. It might mean stepping away from family members, partners, even adult children, leaving careers or moving out of your home.

To choose yourself is to prioritize authenticity over conformity, truth over comfort and personal integrity over external validation. From a young age many of us are conditioned to believe that our worth is tied to how well we meet the expectations of others. We are praised for obedience, for fitting in and for sacrificing our desires, for so called service of the collective good. There is some value in this as they foster co-operation and harmony. Yet they are limiting when they suppress our individuality and stifle our true essence.

The problem is over time we learn to suppress our real needs, ignore our instincts and wear masks that please others, while alienating ourselves from who we really are.

INCONVENIENT CONSCIOUSNESS

To choose yourself is to peel away the layers of conditioning and face the raw unvarnished truth of our inner being. *It requires stepping into the discomfort and inconvenience of self-awareness.* Confronting the parts of ourselves that we have been taught to hide or deny.

This process is not for the feint hearted because it often means challenging the narratives, we have built our lives around. It may mean acknowledging the path we have been walking, however successful or acceptable it appears to be on the outside, does not align with our deepest values and aspirations. It involves knowing our vibration is affected by our environment and it is our magnetism to life. The very essence of our creative abilities.

This act of courage is not without consequences. Choosing yourself can disrupt relationships, challenge societal norms and lead to periods of uncertainty in isolation. This has certainly been my experience. The world around us is often uncomfortable with those of us who choose authenticity over compliance.

The decision to prioritize yourself can be met with resistance, criticism or misunderstanding. It takes immense inner strength to whether these reactions without retreating into the safety of conformity. But the rewards of choosing yourself outweighs the challenges. When we know our true selves, we unlock our full potential. This includes a reservoir of vitality and creativity that can transform not only our lives but also the lives of those around us. By living authentically, we give others the permission to do the same. Our courage becomes a beacon, a reminder that it's possible to live in alignment with our values and dreams even in the face of adversity.

The courage to choose yourself can, and often does, begin in small ways. It may start by saying no, to something that feels wrong or setting a boundary that has been ignored. It might mean speaking the truth that has been silenced for too long or following a passion that has been dismissed or seen as impractical. Although these seem to be small acts, they are revolutionary in their implications. They signal a shift from living according to external dictates, to living in alignment with your own compass.

This inner compass is not always an easy path to follow. It requires you to turn down the noise of the world and instead to listen to the subtle whispers of the soul. In this process you will begin to trust in yourself with a new level of respect as your soul leads you to the life of your dreams.

Choosing yourself does not mean rejecting others or abandoning responsibility. It is not an act of selfishness but of self-respect. It's the recognition that we cannot truly give to others unless we first honour our own needs and desires. When we choose ourselves, we show up in the world as whole integrated beings, capable of offering genuine love and connection.

We are becoming more loving as we let go of fear; we want to come together as a community and to feel oneness. It's happening with greater momentum, with every year that passes. As we question the old paradigm and return to what our human ancestors knew- everything is energy and energy is changeable. The four bodies of the human- physical, mental, emotional and spiritual are energetic. We can heal them ourselves. Healing is about changing your reality to something better. When we change our vibration, we change our reality.

If something feels good and is for the highest good of all, it is being aligned to your highest timeline, life path or mission. This alignment feels good and it's a reminder of our home and who we really are, the joy of existence and our authentic self. We chose to be created for the expansion and the joy of it and the experience of this joy is our birth right.

When we choose to see life through a new lens and live in this new perception, eventually we'll find ourselves back where we came from. This is a conscious homecoming. Our home, being our connection with oneness; with ourselves, with each other, with everything, the Divine. We never energetically, or in truth, ever left home. Thinking we did was a part of the illusion of separation.

Even though there have been some evil influences along the way, this experience of separation has allowed us to fully know ourselves. We are learning about the individual aspect of creation that we are. Unique, precious, miraculous, connected, loved and infinite. Knowing this individual self, but at the same time knowing where we fit in, and our connection to all.

This is the meaning of earthly life. Its purpose is simply to experience as much as we can, which, in turn, expands the universe. There is no wrong or right way to do this, just your unique and individual way and how beautifully creative that uniqueness is. You are the writer, director, producer and the star of the incredible block buster movie. That is your expression of life. Only you can choose when it is time to leave the Karmic path and embrace the Dharmic path.

You can choose if this happens gradually, which is more common, or if it happens rapidly. Only you can limit your brilliance by resisting life, stubbornly holding on to what was, by buying into fears, dramas, limitations and restrictions. That empowering statement is life changing when you really get it! It's up to you! Only you can choose where you focus your attention, if you want to discover who you really are and then decide to give that your undivided attention.

I hope you find within these pages the formula for making this adventurous path flow with surrender and curiosity. Having a road map is an opportunity for more ease and less struggle but nothing is truly guaranteed in life except change. This is your perception, your choice and your life. It will change but the direction of that change is up to you.

If you take just one piece of support with you, let it be this "you are the creator and co-creator of your experiences". It's all you and the perception you choose.

On this earthly adventure we have the choice to uncover our shadow-selves or fearful or wounded-self and own them. If we make the choice to wake up, then everything inauthentic or limited about ourselves and life drops away. And then the fun begins as we discover who we really are: A multi-dimensional spiritual being having a human experience and at this time awakening to our divine blueprint.

This path calls on your perseverance, courage, dedication, unity consciousness, spiritual connection, faith, hope, loving awareness and your ability to trust and self-reflect. And finally, to know and then love all of who you are.

As you move through this journey (in the University of growth often referred to as "The Earth School"), with your intentions towards ascension into our New World or whichever direction or path you choose, I wish you ease and grace along with the courage to surrender to your life's path. Evolution is change and change is inevitable in the universe. All souls here on earth will, at some time, ascend into a higher level of consciousness from where they perceive themselves to be. They will do this in their own time and in their own way, whether that happens this lifetime or in two hundred lifetimes. To me, the nature of the universe is conscious and self-aware and is in a process of never-ending change.

I ask you to consider if this life, this planet that was highjacked eons before this time, has it run its course for you? Now you find yourself here, having *almost* finished this book perhaps pondering, wondering what's next? You are now awake to a new reality, but you can go back to sleep if you want. If you love how things are, if you love this life just as it is and all that goes on here is to your liking, then its highly likely you will do nothing with this information. If this is you? I offer you love and grace for your path and thank you for being open to something different.

If you have been moved in any way by something you read and have recognised some shifts within you or are questioning things that you didn't before, then maybe you have connected with a deeper mission. Or simply have new ideas about how things could be better and perhaps you feel a little unsettled? Not knowing all the answers could be new to you? Just be clear about what your questions are. I promise you; the answers will unfold.

It could be that you have been through many struggles and suffered this lifetime and many other lifetimes and now these experiences have been given meaning and purpose. Maybe you have a more in-depth view of who you really are which opens up new doorways and perceptions.

I'd like to offer you the possibility that if you choose to stay awake it will have its challenges, but they will serve you well. Then there will come a time of great peace and harmony within. In this awakened state you are returning to love, to a place where you can most truly be yourself. This will bring reunion, completion and a sense that you have found where you are meant to be. You can finally feel the home that you longed for, is within you.

And perhaps, above all, I'd like to say to you no matter what you choose, never give up. Never stop. Keep going.

You are worth it, and you will succeed, whatever success means to you. You will know you are home when you know the glory of who you really are, and it will bring tears to your eyes. In that moment you will know heaven is within you and always has been and that you are loved eternally.

You will feel more joy than you can bear, you will feel and be love, not just sometimes but more and more of the time. Your entire life will have changed. You will know everything that you are going through and have been through has brought you to this place. You will know, I am you and you are me and so the love story continues to unfold. Thank you for being here, for following the path of your heart and for sharing this journey.

CHAPTER 9 QUESTIONS:

A) What is "The meaning of life" for you?

B) Is there an area of your life where you struggle to go with the flow of your life's path? How could that be different?

C) Are you choosing yourself or does that present a challenge for you? What if anything, do you want to change about this?

D) How does owning your unconscious beliefs/shadow-self allow you to be less judgemental and more at peace in your life?

E) In what way does knowing more about your pineal gland help you?

F) How will you know when you are on the Karmic path and when you are on the Dharmic path?

G) How content are you with your connection to the Divine?

H) Is there a step you can take on a regular basis to support your own happiness? E.g., setting a daily intention, improving your perception of yourself, setting boundaries, becoming aware of your inner voice and how it's affecting you.

I) When you recognise choosing fear is causing struggle in your life, how will you know you have shifted to choosing love? How can you make that shift?

J) What tools or words are you taking from this book to assist you in your life?

Our New World

A new horizon, a new unsettling, renouncing undertakings of the past,
Unsettling your seat of complacency and bringing all together at last.

Back to a known name and centre, to collaborate self and soul,
What will become you cannot know, as its journey is your making to unfold.

You shall make it be into being, from your intentions and thoughts above all,
As you own your shame, guilt and abhorrence, born from the past and the fall.

You release the old and help birth the new, while receiving blessings from above,
Receiving into yourself the pure heart, of the one who is known by their love.

You capture the rays of the new beginning, like sunlight transmuting to Grace,
It dazzles, empowers and raises you up and allows you to know your true place.

You are the creator of your path, of all you perceive and feel,
That which you wish to create is now here, and you, yes you, make it real.

LORINA

SUMMARY

Our work is to look at those parts of ourselves that we don't want to remember or see. While bringing these times into our heart and lovingly see ourselves in those experiences as we integrate all aspects of who we are. The shift into Ascension is living in this moment and being capable of living adjacent to this old reality. Where you are in flow and non-resistance, so that the dramas happening are not affecting you because you are in harmony with life. Your perception is different, so you experience the world differently. It's like being in two worlds with a perception of one reality.

In times to come it will feel as if the world has split in two, yet you have not gone anywhere. The struggles go on, but you are not in them or of them. Your perception has changed therefore you have changed. You are living in unity consciousness and feel the connection to everyone and the peace this brings. You will create in this world the experience of your own knowing and trust the Divine to walk side by side with you, the hand that is always holding yours. Surprising and delighting you at every turn, showering you with abundance and joy. Always being present for you and with you. The world conforms to you when you trust yourself. The very blanket of divinity rests around you and conforms to the body you are made of, to the circumstances of life you have chosen.

INCONVENIENT CONSCIOUSNESS

The method of ownership and the careful dialogue between yourself and what you are holding in your depths allows this shift to occur. When you relinquish the struggle and are not in resistance but in surrender and flowing, then you see the truth of who you are being revealed in this moment.

When you confront and delve inward to what you have been, from the perspective of one who cherishes all of that, your eyes see only love. As though you are now in this moment in its entirety and can choose for yourself what to extinguish and what to carry forward.

Your path is bright and clear as you walk together with the acceptance of all parts of yourself, and then develop a relationship with your true self, who is both an individual expression and unified with all there is.

This is the shift, often referred to as the Ascension process and moving into the fifth dimension, a love-based reality. You have freewill whether you do it now in this place or do it another time far from here. Whether you put it off indefinitely, move slowly or focus completely on it. Your glorious expression will find your way, as it has and does in every moment of your life.

How extraordinary that you are the only you, anywhere and at any time in all the universes; there is only one you. How precious you are, how important you are to this amazing jigsaw puzzle of life at this time and more than all of this, how loved you are. Please know there are no words, just a boundaryless universe of love for you and of you.

My love and blessings always, in all ways.

www.ingramcontent.com/pod-product-compliance
Lightning Source LLC
Chambersburg PA
CBHW072150070526
44585CB00015B/1078